OBJECT: MATRIMONY

*The Risky Business of Mail-Order Matchmaking
on the Western Frontier*

CHRIS ENSS

TWODOT®

GUILFORD, CONNECTICUT
HELENA, MONTANA
AN IMPRINT OF GLOBE PEQUOT PRESS

A · T W O D O T® · B O O K

Copyright © 2013 by Chris Enss

TwoDot is an imprint of Globe Pequot Press and a registered trademark of Morris Book Publishing, LLC.

Project editor: Meredith Dias
Layout: Joanna Beyer

Library of Congress Cataloging-in-Publication Data

Enss, Chris, 1961-
  Object, matrimony : the risky business of mail-order matchmaking on the Western frontier / Chris Enss.
    p. cm.
  Includes bibliographical references and index.
  ISBN 978-0-7627-7399-2
  1. Marriage brokerage—West (U.S.)—History—19th century. 2. Mail order brides—West (U.S.)—History—19th century. 3. Mail order brides—West (U.S.)—Biography. 4. Frontier and pioneer life—West (U.S.) 5. West (U.S.)—Social life and customs—19th century. I. Title.
  HQ802.E5753 2013
  306.82—dc23

                              2012008293

Printed in the United States of America

10 9 8 7 6 5 4 3 2 1

CONTENTS

Acknowledgments v

Foreword vii

Introduction x

A Wife Wanted 1

Annie Gayle & Horace Knapp 2

The *Matrimonial News* 7

An Unlikely Match 18

Left at the Station 21

Destined for Disappointment 24

The Busy Bee Club 30

Marriage & Money 35

Annie Stephens & Asa Mercer 41

Making Matrimony Pay 48

The Bride & the Hoarder 55

Matrimonial News Features 58

The Murderous Mail-Order Bride 63

The *New Plan Company* Catalog for Matrimony 67

Without Any Courting 78

"I Do" for a Price 83

Edith Collins & William Moore 88

The Business of Marriage 95

Contents

Buying for the Bride 103

The Shifty Matrimonial Agent. 108

Hannah Gould 114

Want-Ad Brides 119

Runaway Brides 125

Fred Harvey 132

Happily Ever After. 137

Afterword 142

Bibliography 146

Index 150

About the Author 154

ACKNOWLEDGMENTS

I have depended constantly upon the advice and encouragement of key individuals and organizations while working on this follow-up book to *Hearts West: True Stories of Mail-Order Brides on the Frontier.* There's no way to adequately thank them, but I'm going to try to do so.

I gratefully acknowledge the generous assistance of Barb Messer at the Madelyn Helling Library in Nevada City for handling the interlibrary loan transactions and for her vigilant effort to get the hard-to-locate material I needed. I wish to thank the library's director, MaryAnn Trygg, for her kindness and sincere interest in whatever subject matter I'm pursuing.

Special thanks are due to John Gonzales and Kathy Correia at the California Historical Library in Sacramento, California; Lori Devanaussi at the Steven H. Hart Library in Denver, Colorado; Fred Poyner at the Washington State Historical Society in Tacoma, Washington; Beverly Hackney at the *Decatur Review* newspaper in Decatur, Illinois; the researchers at the Kansas City Historical Society in Kansas City, Missouri; and the legal staff at Proctor & Gamble for supplying me with family history, letters, photographs, anecdotes, and articles.

I take great pleasure in acknowledging my obligation to Patti Ferree, Jeff Galpin, and the other talented members at House of Print and Copy in Grass Valley, California. I'd be lost without them.

Cathy Reeves, Dodge City (Kansas) Public Library director, contributed greatly to completing this book, and I thank her for her enthusiasm and genuine love of authors.

I am indebted to my creative and hardworking editor, Erin Turner, and appreciative of the long relationship I've had with Globe Pequot Press. I look forward to writing many more books for the publishing house.

FOREWORD

As the prairie and the West were being settled, unmarried men as well as families staked their claim or homestead and began a new life. Single men and widowers were soon seeking a wife, and many began looking for a mail-order bride. These men did not look in the Sears Roebuck and Co. catalog as the term "mail order" might imply, but rather placed ads in magazines and newspapers that circulated throughout the United States (and some beyond). Single women also placed ads in various publications hoping to move west and start a new life. These ads were also showing up in folded double sheets and broadsides devoted entirely to the matrimonial prospects. The *Matrimonial News,* a paper published in San Francisco; Kansas City, Missouri; and London, was an example of a publication designed specifically to run personal ads for those looking for a mate to marry.

The story of mail-order brides began in the mining communities. Very few men struck it rich, but once out west they often decided to stay. As the men took on farming, ranching, or opening businesses, they also wanted to start a family. Since men outnumbered the women, many searched for a wife by placing an ad in one of the available publications. As far as the women were concerned, many in the East were looking for a life that did not include loneliness, poverty, or spinsterhood. Following the Civil War many women were widowed and wanted a spouse. At this time women outnumbered men in the East, so the West was a logical place to look for that husband.

Some sources suggest that by 1865 there were an estimated thirty thousand single women in the East. The substantial number of bachelors in the plains and the West offered them a chance to find a husband. Newspapers from Nebraska, Kansas, and Wyoming began running ads placed by both men and women, such as "A young lady residing in one of the small towns in Central New York is desirous of opening a correspondence with some young man in the West, with a view to a matrimonial engagement. . . . She is about 24 years of age, possesses a good moral character . . . is tolerably well-educated, and thoroughly versed in the mysteries of housekeeping." An ad from a man looking for a wife might read "A Bachelor of 40, good appearance and substantial means, wants a wife. She must be under 30, amiable, and musical."

Letters then were the means of courtship between a bachelor and a prospective bride; people used the written language to persuade someone to become their mate. Men and women could easily misrepresent their physical attributes, their station in life, and even their finances. Photographs may or may not have been exchanged. When the bride arrived at her destination, either the bride or the groom might find that what they were seeking was not what they found. Other times, a ticket sent by a homesteader to his betrothed might get cashed in, and the bride would never arrive. Those who were illiterate would dictate their letters to someone else to write, which might result in a misrepresentation of the unwary correspondent.

Some couples never married, while others did and had long and successful lives together. For still others, the union was not a happy one. In her first book, *Hearts West: True Stories of Mail-Order Brides on the Frontier*, Chris Enss tells the true stories of women who became mail-order brides. In this book, Enss has compiled more stories and information about courageous brides and their exploits. She tells the amusing story of a young widow whose intended did not show up at the train station, as well as recounting ads and stories from the *Matrimonial News*. You will also learn the marriage broker's role in uniting brides and grooms.

Enss's passion for writing about women in the West is evident in her many books. This one continues this theme as she gives us a flavor of the times and insight into what a single woman or widow did to become a bride. As you read the stories and the ads from the publications, you will learn about the lives of single women wanting a husband and family and willing to do what was necessary—including becoming a mail-order bride—to accomplish this goal. Enss once again brings our history to life and lets us feel what these women were experiencing.

Cathy Reeves
Director, Dodge City Library
Dodge City, Kansas

Introduction

When gold was discovered in the far West during the nineteenth century, a billowing mass of humanity swept toward the setting sun with the swiftness of a tidal wave. Prospectors, businessmen, and explorers came seeking a better way of life and with the hope of amassing a fortune. No matter what riches were to be had or the endless territories yet to be conquered, unattached settlers who made the journey longed for a companion to share the new land. Due to the rigors of the frontier, males were in the vast majority. The few women who did migrate to points beyond the Mississippi were laundresses, cooks, pioneers with children, adventurers with no desire to wed, or soiled doves.

The need for marriageable women in the West immediately following the Gold Rush was great. According to the October 6, 1859, edition of the *Daily Alta California* newspaper, it was estimated that there were two hundred men to every woman. At the close of the Civil War, the lack of men in the East was just as pronounced. Capitalizing on that need on both sides of the country were mail-order bride publications. Women and men in search of a spouse placed advertisements and corresponded with individuals they hoped would agree to marry them. The couples could exchange as few as three letters before accepting a proposal. Others chose to write one another for several years before committing their life to the interested party. Prior to 1865, the cost to mail a letter more than 450 miles from where the correspondence originated was twenty-two cents. According to the book *Journal of the Early Republic*, it was expensive to mail a

A thankful, unidentified groom and his mail-order bride on their wedding day in 1891   COURTESY, COLORADO HISTORICAL SOCIETY AULTMAN COLLECTION, SCAN #20008509

letter because of the transportation necessary to get the letter where it needed to go. Letter writers were charged a minimum of six cents per sheet for delivery up to thirty miles away to a maximum of twenty-five cents per sheet for any distance beyond four hundred miles. Many of the mail-order brides were at least that far away.

Women en route to the place where their future husbands were located carried the few personal belongings they owned in a trunk or satchel. An additional dress, bedclothes, lace collars and cuffs (used to wear over an old dress for a Sunday church service), a family Bible, photographs, and a book or two were all they usually brought with them.

Brides who consented to move west to wed endured a difficult journey whether traveling by stage, with a wagon train, or by steamship. The desire to be a wife and have children was so overwhelming that many women happily agreed to make the strenuous 129-day trip from Independence, Missouri, to San Francisco. Wagon trains and stagecoaches were hot and crowded, and the vehicles easily overturned. Sea travel wasn't any more comfortable and could be dangerous as well. Mail-order brides boarding steamships on the East Coast crossed the Strait of Magellan and then ventured up the Pacific for a trip that lasted more than three months. Between 1852 and 1867, 160 steamships burned, 209 blew up, and more than 570 ships hit an obstruction in the water and sank.

The popularity of two mail-order bride publications, *Matrimonial News* and the *New Plan Company* catalog, sparked entrepreneurs to tap into the market and create their own matchmaking venues. All were devoted to the proposition that every man should have a mate. Traditionalists criticized the patrons that employed this unconventional method of selecting a spouse. Prospective brides and grooms defended their decision to court via mail with a quotation that all the matrimonial newspapers and magazines carried: "Correspondence between intelligent young ladies or gentlemen cannot fail to sharpen the wits and brighten the intellect and is an excellent discipline for the mind. It is an educator in many ways, and the practice of friendly letter writing should be encouraged."

More than 160 years after the first mail-order bride, the same method of choosing a life partner is still being used by some. *Object: Matrimony* contains stories of the origin of the practice and the romantic unions that came about as a result, as well as the disappointments and desertions.

A Wife Wanted

"I am a man of wealth and position," said the widower Shyon Brane to the marriage broker, "and I seek a suitable mate. She must be handsome, cleanly, economical, industrious, and virtuous, a good cook she must be, a thrifty buyer, a capable housekeeper, and not easily stressed. She must know something of music and the arts, dance well and be able to discourse intelligently on history and philosophy withal, she must be cheerful and of affectionate disposition."

"Lo," said the marriage broker, "you come too late. One thousand years ago there was such a paragon but the gods took her to keep house for them. There is no wife for you, but the employment agency can supply you with a dozen domestics who, in a measure, may meet your demands."

—Article placed in the *Santa Fe New Mexican*, Santa Fe, New Mexico, March 9, 1920

Annie Gayle & Horace Knapp

The Dreamer & the Lothario

Annie Gayle was considered one of the prettiest, most ambitious girls in Akron, Ohio. Her eyes were large, her features were well proportioned, and her desire to go west was her number-one aspiration. She was well on her way to achieving her goal when she accepted the proposal of a man living in French Camp, California. He had advertised for an adventurous woman anxious to settle in the Gold Country and experience the excitement of the wild frontier. Annie wasted no time favorably responding to his letter asking for her hand in marriage.

Born an only child in 1874 to Charles Gayle and Margaret Stantz Gayle, Annie grew up hearing her father's tales of the land beyond the Rockies and the endless possibilities to be had there. Charles died before he realized his own dream of moving to San Francisco. Fearing that the chance to make such a journey had died with her father, Annie decided to consider mail-order bride opportunities.

Horace Knapp, a handsome man in his late forties, collected his teenage bride-to-be at the train depot in Sacramento, California, on September 10, 1890. Annie was anxious to meet the sheepish suitor who had described himself in his letters as a "good fellow, with means and prospects." The plan was for the two to marry the day after Annie arrived—and only if their first encounter proved to be mutually satisfactory. The couple dined together and discussed their possible future. By the end of the evening they were in complete accord to wed. Vows and a ring were exchanged the following morning.

Annie was delighted not only to be married, but also finally to be at a location that seemed bursting with potential. If she had remained in Ohio working at a millinery shop, life as a farmer's wife was the best she thought she could hope for. She believed being Mrs. Knapp would bring her happiness, and she therefore surrendered to her husband the small amount of money she had earned working as a seamstress in Akron. It never crossed her mind that Horace might be untrustworthy. She was honest and thought everyone else was as well.

The newlyweds moved to a small cabin nestled in a mining community in the San Juan Valley. Everything went along nicely. It was as though the couple had been settled for years in their new position. Horace invested his wife's funds in a mining venture he explained to her would produce great dividends—enough for them to see the world beyond California. Annie was thrilled by the idea, and while her husband was away tending to their interests, she planned trips to distant lands.

One night, as she sat alone again in their fledgling homestead, a ragged little boy arrived at the doorstep and delivered a soiled note to her. It read as follows:

Mrs. Knapp, your husband has another wife living not far from you. He has three children whom he has deserted. He married you to get whatever money you had or could acquire. She is innocent and knows nothing of him having married you. Don't bother her, poor thing; she has a hard enough time to feed her babies.

Annie was stunned by the news and refused to believe it was true. She tucked the note in her pocket and waited for Horace to arrive home. When Horace finally returned, he walked into the house dressed in a new suit of clothing and a hat and was swinging a cane as though he was in a parade. He carelessly threw himself into a chair and asked Annie if there was anything to eat. For a moment she couldn't speak. If the note was right, she stood to lose her husband, her honor, and the little bit of fortune she had turned over to Horace.

She started to speak, but her tongue was stuck to the roof of her mouth. Horace stared at his bride of a week, waiting for her to reply. Annie didn't say a word; she simply handed him the letter and watched his face. It turned white, then red, then white again. "It's a lie," he said with an oath, "a lie." Annie couldn't stand the terrible strain of the ordeal any further. She fainted and fell on the floor. When she recovered, she was alone. Horace was gone.

He did not appear again for a day or two. In the meantime the once obliging, trusting bride had utterly changed. She was bold and defiant now. She felt the story was true and was determined to make the guilty man pay. He had shown her no mercy in any way, and she would have none for him.

When he finally returned to her, Annie seemed the same as usual. Horace was surprised and couldn't understand it. Her quiet demeanor led him to believe she had resigned herself to the situation. However, she watched him with a careful eye, like a cat watches a mouse. Her apparent resignation completely disarmed him. He was curious as to what was going on.

One evening he went out. Shortly after Horace left, Annie secretly followed him. Wearing a shawl around her head and walking somewhat slumped over, Annie kept a safe distance behind Horace. Past one corner and around another he went until finally he turned onto a small street. His "shadow" followed behind him into a dilapidated building and up a flight of wooden stairs. He stopped at a door at the top of the stairs, paused, turned the knob and entered. Annie was at the keyhole almost before the door was closed.

Annie heard enough to confirm her worst fears. She descended the stairs and rushed home. The next morning, bright and early, she paid a call to the house. A woman in a calico wrapper opened the door for her. Three small children were in the room. "I am Mrs. Horace Knapp," she said in answer to Annie's first question. "Yes, my husband was here. Am I sure? Oh, yes. See here is the photograph." As she spoke she reached behind a clock on a mantel and produced a picture to show the poor girl. It was Horace.

Trembling, Annie removed a locket from around her neck. She opened it to reveal Horace's picture and told the woman her story. The wife was more than indignant. She vowed that Horace should go to jail. He had permitted their children and her to nearly starve, and they were all still very hungry.

Annie returned to her home and met the man who had caused her such misery. Having anticipated trouble, he merely shrugged his shoulders. "Better make the best of it," he said. That night he came home leading a little four-year-old by the hand. "This is my daughter," he said. "I lied to you, but she has to live here now. Her mother met me on the road with two other brats, and raised such a fuss that I agreed to take this one and care for it."

"I will not stay here nor have your children to look after," Annie cried. "I have been enough of a fool already."

The reply so enraged Horace that he grabbed up a carving knife and, brandishing it before Annie's eyes, shouted, "Do what I ask or I will kill you!"

Annie hurried out of the cabin, and Horace chased after her. She lost the furious man in the dark. She reported the incident to the authorities, and Horace was arrested and held on a $1,000 bond. He was charged with bigamy and assault with intent to kill. Annie and Horace's first wife were present at his trial. He was convicted and led away to prison. He was never heard from by either woman or his children again.

Horace's first wife eventually married again. Annie moved to Denver, Colorado, and married again as well. According to the *Daily Alta California* newspaper, which covered the tragic story of the mail-order bride, the second time around both women wed men with "sound morals and good character."

The *Matrimonial News*

Marriage is such an ancient institution, and has in all ages excited such universal interest among the human family, that in offering to the public a journal especially devoted to the promotion of marital facility, we feel sure we are only supplying a national want.

—Leslie Fraser Duncan, Editor/Owner,
Matrimonial News, 1870

The matrimonial wants and needs of single men and women were specifically addressed in a unique newspaper published throughout the 1870s, '80s, and '90s called the *Matrimonial News*. The paper's editorial "statement of purpose" was to "promote marriage and conjugal felicity." Bachelors and spinsters who had no friends or acquaintances from among whom they could choose a life partner turned to the *News* to help them remedy their predicament.

The publication contained thousands of advertisements from people of both sexes and all ages and with annual incomes ranging from $12 to $500,000. The number of handsome young men without means and very fair but penniless women who wished to have their burden of life assuaged by another's comfort was endless. Relied on by many to fulfill these dreams, the *News* flourished for decades.

The paper was established in England in 1870 by entrepreneur Leslie Fraser Duncan. The publication was an instant success. Advertisers throughout the country and in the United States competed for space in the unique and widely read paper.

An unidentified woman poses for an ad in the mail-order bride publication *Matrimonial News* 1890–1905.   COURTESY, COLORADO HISTORICAL SOCIETY AULTMAN COLLECTION, SCAN #20009124

Some community leaders blasted the paper, calling it "silly" and its readers "gullible and naïve." Sir Richard Malin, a vice-chancellor of England's high court, voiced his displeasure over the paper outside of a London courthouse in May 1877. "In looking over the advertisements I found ladies representing themselves as young, attractive, and possessed of considerable property, advertising for husbands, and men, in equally good positions, advertising for wives," he noted. "I can't believe that such advertisements could be other than false and fraudulent in their character. . . . Such a publication was a public nuisance which deserved to be put down."

Leslie Duncan defended his creation in the Letters to the Editor section of the paper. "Civilization combined with the cold for

Portrait of an unidentified woman for *Matrimonial News* 1890–1905
COURTESY, COLORADO HISTORICAL SOCIETY AULTMAN COLLECTION, SCAN #20009120

maladies of society and the rules of etiquette impose such restrictions on the sexes," he wrote. "There are thousands of marriageable
men and women of all ages, capable of making each other happy,
who never have a chance of meeting, either in town or country;
therefore the desirability of unifying some or all using such a

product through which ladies and gentlemen aspiring to marriage can be honorably brought into communication, is too obvious to need demonstration."

In the early days of the paper's existence, widows, clergymen, professional gentlemen, officers, officers' daughters, and doctors made up the bulk of individuals who advertised for a spouse. As time went on miners, farmers, schoolmarms, and seamstresses sponsored the majority of the ads. Many of the widows would describe themselves to readers as "moderately stout," and the professional gentlemen characterized themselves as "well fixed in finances."

Some people who submitted a need in the personal columns were honest and blunt. One youthful widow admitted that she was "not very pretty." Those with very peculiar tastes in a future mate made their ideas known as well. An advertisement that appeared in a summer edition of the *Matrimonial News* illustrated the odd desires of a twenty-eight-year-old woman named Magdaleen. "To Ugly Gentlemen," the ad specified, "I am of prepossessing appearance, and loving, confiding disposition, wishing for a husband described as above. Must be interesting and refined. No cold-hearted gentlemen need apply, whatever may be his position or fortune."

Men, too, had very definite ideas as to what they were looking for in a wife. One businessman of Irish decent requested that no woman under the age of twenty-five respond to his advertisement. He described himself as an "heir of an old country family, age 22, 5 foot 5 inches, dark, very handsome eyes, a poet, highly talented passionately fond of science and the arts, and of beauty in every shape. Is looking to meet a lady of good family and is handsome. . . ."

A year after the *Matrimonial News* was established in London, offices were opened in San Francisco, California, and Kansas City, Missouri. The weekly paper was sold as far east as Albany,

The Kansas City edition of *Matrimonial News* published photographs of prospective brides and grooms like these unidentified men and women.   CHRIS ENSS COLLECTION

New York, and as far west as the Sandwich Islands. Paperboys on street corners in major western cities like Denver, Colorado, and Seattle, Washington, would sell copies of the paper to interested parties. "*Matrimonial News! Matrimonial News!*" the boys would call out in a loud voice. The July 5, 1889, edition of the *Jewish Standard* reported on one instance in which a paperboy in San Francisco stopped a potential customer passing by and asked him if he wanted to buy a copy of the *Matrimonial News*.

"Here, sir," the lad said, touching the man's arm. "This will tell you where to get a wife."

"Thank you," the man replied, "but I already have a wife."

"Then have another, sir. Have another then," the boy prompted cheerfully, offering up a paper.

The American version of the newspaper provided readers with instructions on how to submit an ad and the cost for the ad.

Fair and gentle reader, can we be useful to you? Are you a stranger desiring a helpmate or searching for agreeable company that may in the end ripen into closer ties? If so, send us a few lines making known your desires. Are you bashful and dread publicity? Be not afraid. You need not disclose to us your identity. Send along your correspondence accompanied by five cents for every seven words, and we will publish it under an alias and bring about correspondence in the most delicate fashion. To cultivate the noble aim of life and help men and women into a state of bliss is our aim.

A code of rules and regulations, posted in each edition of the paper, was strictly enforced. All advertisements must give personal appearance, height, weight, financial and social position in life, and a general description of the kind of persons the writer desired to correspond with. Gentlemen's personals of forty words or under were published once for twenty-five cents in stamps or postage.

Ladies' personals of forty words or under were published free of charge. Any advertisement over forty words, whether for ladies or gentlemen, was charged a rate of one cent for each word. Personal advertisements were numbered to avoid the necessity for publishing names and addresses. Replies to personals were to be sent to the *Matrimonial News* office, sealed in an envelope with the number of the ad on the outside.

Every edition of the *Matrimonial News* began with the same positive affirmation: "Women need a man's strong arm to support her in life's struggle, and men need a woman's love."

The following are samples of advertisements that appeared in the January 8, 1887, edition of the Kansas City printing of the *Matrimonial News*.

226 – I am a jolly little girl of 17, with black hair and eyes and fair complexion, weigh 115 pounds, am fond of company and would like to form the acquaintance of a nice gentleman or two with whom I could spend an occasional evening socially, and, if mutually agreeable, become friends with proclivities tending ultimately to the great ambition of women.

219 – Is there a gentleman from 30 to 45 years of age, weighing 170 to 200 pounds, measuring 5 feet and 10 inches up, honorable and intelligent that desires a good wife and housekeeper. Let them answer this number. I can give particulars, photo and best of references if required. Christian preferred.

220 – A good looking young lady of 19, 5 feet 3 inches high, black hair and eyes, would like to find someone to love.

282 – A widower, merchant and stockman, lives in Kansas, 46 years old, height 6 feet, weight 210 pounds, brunette, black hair and eyes, wishes to correspond with ladies of same age,

Neatly coiffed and wearing his finest suit, an unidentified man almost smiled for his ad in *Matrimonial News* in 1891.

without encumbrances and with means, must move in the best society and be fully qualified to help make a happy home: object, matrimony.

279 – I am 27 years of age, a stranger in the city, but shall remain here until winter: I am 5 feet 9 inches tall, weight 150 pounds, in good business and would like to correspond with a good girl who will honor me with her company to theater occasionally. Need list of references as to character, etc.

257 – Wanted someone to love, who will be true and sweet, and not only a darling dove, but truly a wise helpmate. She must be of noble birth, whose worth could not be told, as misers count that sordid worth, of stocks and bonds and gold.

268 – Two good looking young men in a Missouri town, having money at their disposal would be pleased to correspond with two jolly young ladies. Object a quality time and its results.

233 – Answer to 82 - There is a lad in Missouri with a foot that's flat, with seeds in his pocket and a brick in his hat, with an eye that is blue and a No. 10 shoe - he's the "Bull of the Woods" and the boy for you.

266 – I want to know some pretty girl of 17 to 20 years. I am 29, 5 feet 9 inches tall, a blonde: I can laugh for fifteen minutes and I want some pretty girl to laugh with me.

252 – I move in the best society, am 28 years of age, weight 168 pounds, height 5 feet 8 inches, light complexion, heavy mustache, and would like to correspond with some young lady, object matrimony.

214 – Respectable young man, with good position in city, 20 years old, desires the acquaintance of a modest young lady, between the ages of 17 and 21, with home nearby. Object: to attend operas and church; perhaps more.

229 – I am a widower 5 feet 7 inches, 35 years old, weight 150 pounds. I am merrily disposed and would like to make the acquaintance of some honorable lady 30 to 35 years, who would like to share a pleasant home, a kind companion, widow preferred.

173 – A lady, tall, young and handsome, wishes to marry and have a home of her own; she is amiable, and would make a bright and happy home for any man.

202 – A gentlemen of good family, age 25, tall, and good looking, only partner in a good City firm, will be glad to meet with a lady of means with a view to marriage.

169 – A lady, 22, tall, fair, and very handsome, with $500 a year, wishes to marry.

214 – A gentlemen, aged 60, very tall, with more than average good appearance, genial temper, and who believes he could make any reasonable woman happy want to marry. He has an income of some thousands a year, handsome town and country residence, keeps several horses and carriages, and would make a good husband.

297 – Maudie, 19 years of age, beautiful girl, medium height, fair, blue eyes, exquisite and well defined features, amiable disposition, and talented, would make a loving wife, desires to correspond with a young gentlemen aged about 23 of medium height, not stout, brown hair and moustache, must have a knowledge of foreign languages, money no object.

314 – I am a young man, 29 years of age nearly six feet in height, weight 170 lbs., have light hair and mustache, blue eyes and florid complexion. I am by occupation a mechanical engineer, with a steady position at $3500 a year, and have a bank account of $10,000. I have a college education and am a man of refined tastes.

I was born in America and have lived here all my life, and expect to die here. I am looking for an eager woman would like to be a wife and have children. I am looking for someone who wants to live a respectable life and be an ornament to society.

The editors at the *Matrimonial News* believed that for every lonely soul there was a wanting heart. Ads placed in the popular publication helped save many singles from a solitary fate.

An Unlikely Match

From 1875 to 1895, hopeful men and women from Connecticut to California perused the pages of the *Matrimonial News* daily in search of someone who would commit to them for the rest of their lives. Many of the advertisements emphasized a desire to correspond with interested parties for a set time before agreeing to meet in person. Others were willing to promise themselves to the first individual to respond to their notice. Some people scanned the announcements in search of an individual who could improve their financial situation.

In the spring of 1890, a San Francisco bank clerk who also was a dedicated reader of the *Matrimonial News* was convinced he could find a spouse that would meet his economic criteria. He had vowed to locate a woman who had money of her own and who was willing to share. He earned a modest sum of $300 a year and believed he could not support himself and a wife on that salary. He believed in the adage, "It's just as easy to marry a rich woman as a poor one." The clerk argued with his friends who felt he was superficial for thinking that large sums of money made life more comfortable. He told them it was "easier to sit down to a good hot dinner than to have only a cold leg of mutton between him and his wife."

After diligently reviewing the paper, the enterprising clerk found the advertisement he had hoped he'd find. It read, "A lady with a good income living in her own villa charmingly situated, would correspond with a gentleman with a view to matrimony. Bankers preferred. Address with editor." The bank clerk envisioned

An unidentified mail-order bride and groom pose with their wedding party after having exchanged vows in Sacramento, CA, in 1895. COURTESY OF THE CALIFORNIA HISTORY ROOM, CALIFORNIA STATE LIBRARY, SACRAMENTO, CA, SCAN #20093278

himself living in a lavish home and being waited on by a myriad of servants. He quickly responded to the ad, and arrangements were made for the pair to meet over the Easter holiday.

The meeting was to take place at the *Matrimonial News* office in London. Leslie Fraser Duncan, the newspaper's editor, demanded the bank clerk pay him a fee to be introduced to the woman of means about whom he had been fantasizing. Once the money changed hands, Duncan locked it in a safe and led the way to the room where the lady who had placed the advertisement was waiting. The clerk quickly smoothed down his suit and slicked back his hair. The woman, whose back was to the pair when they entered, was dressed in yards of crimson and black taffeta. She also wore a huge hat complete with feathers and a veil that covered her face.

The woman turned to greet the bank clerk, and his first thought was that she "evidently wished to make up in dress for what she lacked in youth." The woman peeled back the veil as Duncan announced, "Miss Montgomery Jones, allow me to introduce . . ." Before he could complete the introduction, the woman let out a bloodcurdling scream and then fainted. The men rushed to Miss Jones's aid, and it was then the clerk fully realized the reason for her unexpected reaction. Miss Jones was the bank clerk's maiden maternal aunt.

Neither the clerk nor his aunt had used their real names to place or answer their advertisements.

Left at the Station

A lively, petite woman with dark hair and dark eyes coaxed a pair of blonde mares pulling a well-used buggy toward a train depot in Taylorsville, Texas. When the vehicle reached the building, she tugged on the reins, and the horses came to a quick stop. Nine curious men waiting on the platform and carefully eyed her every move.

According to the March 19, 1898, edition of the *Daily Light* newspaper in San Antonio, Texas, the men were waiting for the narrow gauge to arrive and transport them all to Davisburg. The last thing they expected to encounter was the very high-spirited, gregarious Widow Jones.

Carrying a stack of letters bound together with a blue ribbon, she approached each man and studied his face carefully. "Are you Mr. John Hope?" she inquired of them one at a time. They all told her no, and when she had passed the last one, she came back to one of the men dressed in uniform. His rank was that of colonel. The widow sat down on a bag of fertilizer land-plaster and took a photograph from her pocket and said, "That's the man I'm after, but it seems he hasn't showed up."

"Your husband, ma'am?" queried the colonel.

"Not jest yit, sah. He was to be if he had got here today, and we liked the looks of each other, but I guess he's backed out. What sort of galoot would you take him to be?"

"I shouldn't like to pass an opinion on a friend of yours."

"Oh, you needn't mind that," replied the woman, as she shifted the bags beside her. "Would you say he was a squar' man? He lives over at Gordonsville, and we've been correspondin' by mail. He was to be here today to marry me, but he'd flunked right out. Does he look like a flunk to you?"

"Well, ma'am," said the colonel, after a good look at the photograph, "he may be a good man or a bad one. I wouldn't want to do him an injustice, you know."

"Is his nose sat on right?"

"It's a pretty fair nose."

"Is he too wide between the eyes?"

"Perhaps, not."

"How's his mouth?"

"Really, my dear woman, you must excuse me," said the colonel, as he returned the photograph. "You see . . ."

"Yes, I see," interrupted the woman, as she received it. "I see I'm a widder and he's a widder fur five years. This feller puts an ad in a paper for a wife, I send him a picture; he falls in love with me and writes me over fifty love letters. I finally give him my heart. He is to be here on the train to marry me. He don't show up. I am left. What is to be done about it?"

"I . . . I don't know, ma'am," stammered the colonel.

"Are you married?"

"Yes'm."

"All the others married?"

"All married," the men replied in chorus.

"Then I tell you what is to be done about it!" she explained, as she rose up and flourished the switch around. "I git into my buggy and drive back home. I stand on a stump in the front yard and blow the dinner horn. About fifteen different fellers who want to marry the Widder Jones will come gallopin' down the road and across lots and the prize, and Mr. John Hope of Gordonsville kin go to grass and be hanged to him! That's me, and that's my way, and if any of you want to kiss the bride, now's your golden opportunity."

Exactly what happened after the Widow Jones made the bold announcement was not noted. The reporter for the *Daily Light* speculated that the men were too stunned to respond. They boarded the train as soon as it arrived, and the widow—and jilted mail-order bride—returned to her buggy and drove off into the countryside.

Destined for Disappointment

Deacon Joe Sleet's correspondence with the widow Nellie Wallace was full of promise for the future. When they began writing one another in late 1925, Mrs. Wallace had hoped to find a man who would love and care for her as her deceased husband once had. When she placed an ad in the Get Acquainted section of a western magazine and the deacon responded, she believed he was the answer to her heart's longing. "I'm not a flapper," her advertisement read, "but I would like to exchange letters with a man between the age of twenty-five and thirty-two. I want a husband good and true, there is a chance it might be you," the notice concluded.

Twenty-two-year-old Nellie Wallace lived in Tchula, Mississippi, 1,500 miles from Joe Sleet's home in El Paso, Texas. Of all the letters she received in reply to her ad, Joe's struck her fancy completely. In a short time Nellie was writing Joe to the exclusion of anyone else. Through his letters she learned that he was a deacon in the Baptist church and that he was a widower. Nellie confided in him that she too was the victim of a sad romance, her husband having died some years ago.

The correspondence was hardly a month old before Joe had been granted permission to call his fair correspondent "Sweetheart." Another week and respective photographs were exchanged; still another and a row of *x*'s appeared at the bottom of their letters. Another month passed and more letters were delivered at the Sleet home. In one of those letters Nellie admitted there was a "spark of love aglow" in her heart.

The fervor of the letters increased with their frequency. Then came the inevitable exchange of locks of hair, with Nellie giving an accurate description of herself. She informed Joe she was five feet, eight inches tall, weighed 180 pounds but, being tall, did not look obese. "And goodness knows," the account concluded, "I like to eat." Her devotion to the truth did not quench the flame of Joe's growing love for Nellie. "Sweetheart," he replied, "your age, weight, hair, eyes, and everything is all right with me if you will only make some suggestion about the 'yes' part of it. Say 'yes' now, Nellie. Your loving Joe."

Nellie's letter back to Joe included the answer he had pleaded for. He was elated, and he sent a note back to her telling of his joy. In this ecstatic note Joe drew a picture of his heart with heart-shaped teardrops falling from it. "Now you can see," was the accompanying comment, "that my heart belongs to you." He signed his letter "Your All-the-Time Valentine."

At a later date Joe sent another letter detailing what train Nellie needed to take to get to him and what was to happen once she arrived in Texas.

> We will be married at my home the night you arrive. I live with my mother. I am keeping our plans a secret from the pastor. I will tell him on Sunday that I am going to call a deacon's meeting at my home on Thursday night and that the three deacons and I want him to be present. He will think it is just a regular business meeting until he finds out that one of his deacons wants him to officiate the happiest occasion of his life.

It was with that rosy promise and the anticipation of a joyous future that Nellie caught the next train for El Paso. The ceremony came off on schedule, and Nellie, happy to escape bachelor girlhood, joyous in her newfound love, thought that her life couldn't get any happier. However, her happiness was short-lived.

The first real problem between Nellie and Joe started with Joe's mother. She did not like Nellie and was not shy about showing it. The two women could not agree on anything and were vocal about it. Furthermore, the groom had been led to believe, because of Nellie's acknowledged fondness of food, that she would be able to make lavish meals. Joe was doomed to disappointment. Within a month the disgruntled bridegroom, fed up with the bickering and lack of home-cooked meals by his wife, quietly disappeared one day. Joe's mother broke the news to her daughter-in-law that her new spouse had moved to Chicago.

Nellie was humiliated and furious. She moved to a neighbor's house and began making plans to divorce Joe. In the meantime she found a job as a caretaker for an elderly woman. Joe beat Nellie in filing for a divorce, citing as his reasons that his mail-order bride had refused to cook his meals, fought with his mother, threatened his mother's life, and demanded that his mother leave. Nellie quickly countersued on the grounds of desertion. According to the October 5, 1926, edition of the *El Paso Times,* Nellie was mortified by Joe's accusation. "I don't want him anymore," she told a *Times* reporter. "And I wouldn't live with him, but I am determined to go to court and to show him up."

Meanwhile, the deacon sadly thought over his broken dreams and put himself on record with the *Times* as being through with mail-order matrimony. "I found out a month after the wedding," he affirmed, "that our marriage was a mistake. I tried to get my wife to go back to her own mother. She refused. She wanted us to get a house to ourselves. I could not afford to do that. There was no use trying to reason with her. I left El Paso for Alexandria, Louisiana, my old home, where I remained a week. I did not leave her, as she claims, penniless. There was a deposit of $75 in the State National Bank, which was available for a ticket to Tchula, Mississippi."

The divorce case took time to prepare. Meanwhile, the congregation of the church where Joe served was divided in their feelings and greatly concerned over the matter. There were those that sided with the bride and those who declared themselves to be loyal supporters of the deacon.

During a Sunday morning service directly following the announcement of the official breakup of the newlyweds, the atmosphere was electric with unvoiced opinion. The bride and groom sat on opposite sides of the church, and members of the congregation who had taken a side in the matter sat with the person they believed had the most legitimate case.

When the case finally came to trial, thousands of El Paso residents flooded the courtroom to hear the outcome of the troubled marriage between the deacon and his mail-order bride. The Sleets' divorce was finalized on October 1, 1926.

Nellie and Joe Sleet's mail-order marriage wasn't the only correspondence romance that ended in bitter divorce. In 1914, Leola McGover from Excelsior Springs, Missouri, waited patiently to walk down the aisle of the Methodist church in Silver City, Idaho, and exchange vows with Lawrence Woodring, a miner who was living in Silver City. The couple had met via an advertisement Lawrence posted in the *New Plan Company* catalog. He was searching for a wife, and Leola answered the call. They corresponded for more than two years before Lawrence proposed. The date of June 14, 1914, was set for the wedding. The interesting outcome of the much-anticipated event made the Town Talk section of the *Coeur d'Alene Press*. According to the article dated June 22, the wedding between Leola and Lawrence was to be an "elegant event." Among the bridesmaids was a cousin from Kansas City, Missouri. The groom and the cousin got along very well and the bride-to-be was pleased. Leola wanted her husband to like all the members of her family.

On the day of the wedding the church was packed with relatives and friends of both families. "The intended bride was beautiful in her marriage garb," the Town Talk article read. "She was as happy as any girl has a right to be. Suddenly the blow fell. It was a horrible blow. It came from a note—a note from the man who was to have been her husband within the hour."

"Leola," the note began, "I'm sorry, but there's nothing else that I can do. Your cousin and I fell madly in love the moment we looked at each other. Our happiness lies together. And if I married you I would put a curse on both our lives. Please do your best to forgive me."

Leola was stunned by the revelation and fainted. Lawrence and his former fiancée's cousin traveled to Kansas City, Missouri, where they were married shortly thereafter. Leola left Idaho and settled in San Francisco.

The five brides of George Stevens experienced similar shock and dismay when they learned the man they wed was married to several others. From 1929 to 1932, sixty-three-year-old Stevens used the matrimonial agency the American Friendship Society to find a suitable partner to marry. Stevens was a traveling shoe salesman for the Stride Rite Shoe Company based out of Cincinnati, Ohio.

According to the May 21, 1932, edition of the Hutchinson, Kansas, newspaper the *Hutchinson Daily News*, Stevens told representatives at the five different American Friendship Society offices across the state of Ohio that "he was lonely and needed a faithful wife." The society was successful in matching Stevens with just such women. After exchanging a few letters with Blanche Burch of Athens, Ohio, Lulu Burke of Plainwell, Cora Hamilton of Union City, Utha Liggett of Margurette Springs, and Mary Endres of Oberlin, he arranged to meet them. Not long after their initial meetings, he proposed and quickly married. After each wedding he spent about a month with his bride and then departed with whatever cash or jewelry of theirs he could make off with.

Lulu Burke was the first to report Stevens to Plainwell's police. He deserted her in October 1931, taking $11 in cash and her checkbook. It wasn't until Utha Liggett came forward to report that her husband stole $800 from her that the authorities noticed a similarity in the crimes and the description of Stevens. By reviewing teletypes exchanged between police forces, statewide law enforcement was able to identify the accused as the same man. Further investigation showed that Stevens was married not only to Burke and Liggett, but also to three other women.

Steven was arrested at a hotel room in Cincinnati, Ohio, on May 2, 1932, and charged with bigamy and theft.

The Busy Bee Club

Free Women of the West

Wanted: A nice, plump, healthy, good natured, good look-
ing domestic and affectionate lady to correspond with. Object
- matrimony. She must be between 22 and 35 years of age.
She must be a believer in God and immortality, but no sectar-
ian. She must not be a gad-about or given to scandal, but must
be one who will be a helpmate and companion, and who will
endeavor to make a happy home. Such a lady can find a cor-
respondent by addressing the editor of this paper. Photographs
exchanged!
—William J. Berry's advertisement in the Yuma,
Arizona, *Sentinel*, 1875

It was 1879, and the nightlife in the mining town of Tombstone,
Arizona Territory, was in full swing. The burg's main thoroughfare
featured a string of saloons and bathhouses filled to capacity with
thirsty citizens. A dirty, unshaven miner walked down the street
past a row of the rowdy businesses carrying a loaded six-shooter
in his hand. The angry man glowered at bystanders who dared to
stand in his way. Nothing was going to stop him from his violent
mission.

He entered the Occidental Bar and scanned the sea of faces, looking for his prey. A thick haze of cigarette and cigar smoke hovered over the dingy, crowded room. The man glanced down at his gun and then made his way along the bar.

A young woman with ebony skin and smooth black hair sat at the end of the counter next to a large man with heavy jowls, a round face, and a straggly mustache. His hands were all over the woman's body, and she giggled as he kissed her neck. The miner raised his weapon, pointed it at the fat man, and pulled the hammer back. Frightened saloon patrons scattered.

The fat man jumped up and stumbled away from the bar. The miner followed his every move with the barrel of his gun. The young woman was undaunted, as if she had witnessed this kind of display before. She smiled a sphinxlike smile at the miner and stepped out of the way. "I saw her first," he snarled at the fat man. The fat man quickly reached for his gun. KABLAAAMM!! KABLAAAMM!! When the shooting stopped, the fat man lay dead on the floor, two bullets in his chest.

Scenes like this played out over and over again in the Old West. With too few women to go around, and prostitutes setting up business, married African-American women living in mining camps around Tucson, Arizona Territory, sought to put an end to violent behavior and ultimately bring social reform to the unruly black communities. In 1885, six wives, convinced the problem was the lack of marriageable women in the area, met to arrange mail-order brides for Arizona miners. They called their enterprising group the Busy Bee Club.

Members of the Busy Bee Club ran advertisements in newspapers and wrote letters to churches in the East inviting single women to come west. Lured by opportunities offered in the wild territories, many women responded to the call. Candidates mired in poverty, family problems, or personal tragedies hoped to begin life anew on the frontier. Before those hoping to find love and happiness were

FEMALE CLUBS vs. MATRIMONY.

Miss Firebrace—"SEND YOUR HORSE HOME, AND STOP AND DINE HERE WITH ME, JULIA! I'VE ASKED TRIXY RATTLECASH AND EMILY SHEP-PARD."
Mrs. Bolingbroke Tompkins, nee Julia Wildrake with a sigh of regret for the freedom of Spinsterhood and the charms of Club life)—"CAN'T, MY DEAR GIRL! MY SAINTED OLD FATHER-IN-LAW'S JUST GONE BACK TO CHICAGO, AND POOR BOLLY'S ALL ALONE!"

This cartoon, which ran in *Punch* magazine in 1900, pokes fun at spinsters and clubs that promote the so-called joys of being single.

given a one-way ticket west, they had to consent to marry the miner who selected each as his bride on sight. This condition was not a big concession in the eyes of these women, and they quickly agreed to it.

Black miners throughout the West anxiously awaiting the women's arrival discussed how they would decide on the selection of brides. Even though all the men had contributed financially to the endeavor, seniority won out, and the oldest men gained the right to choose first. Some of the men were old enough to be fathers and grandfathers of the teenagers they selected to marry. More often than not, the mail-order brides were second wives for the senior miners who had lost their first wives. These men had large families and needed help caring for them. Once the vows were exchanged, the naive young women took on a houseful of children as well as a husband.

On rare occasions these mail-order brides were treated to elaborate weddings. Miner Thomas Detter of Eureka, Nevada, gave his betrothed, Emily Brinson, a splendid ceremony complete with a gift of diamond earrings and a gold wedding band. According to the *Eureka Sentinel,* their ceremony, held in June of 1876, was "attended by nearly all of the colored folks in town, besides some twenty-five or thirty white people, including some of our most prominent citizens and their wives."

Another such extravagant ceremony took place in San Francisco in 1867. Sara Anderson and Wellington Patrick married under a canopy of chiffon, and the bride was ushered in by the Black Pacific Brass Band. Brides on the other end of the spectrum considered their ceremony to be a posh affair if their grooms stepped down off their horse to exchange vows. According to the *Daily Alta California* newspaper in February of 1867, one couple took their vows without leaving their saddles. A couple named James and Belle rode up on horseback before a justice of the peace and said their "I do's" atop their rides. James asked the justice of the peace, "Can you marry us?"

"Well, yes," the justice responded, "I guess I can swear you and that gal to support each other. Join hands. Stranger do you swear that you believe that the gal whose hand you are holding, you will support as long as you breathe?" the justice asked. James agreed to do so, and his betrothed took the same pledge. The justice concluded the ceremony with "I now call you one. Farewell."

There were some African-American women who immigrated to California for the sole purpose of living an independent life. But no sooner had they arrived than many found themselves the subject of a prearranged marriage. Friends and relatives of single black women expected them to be engaged within days of their arrival west. Suitors paid well-meaning matchmakers handsomely to wed the unencumbered females. Out of fear of being killed by the suitors, most women went along with the arrangement.

The widow Pauline Williamson took exception to this practice and shunned attempts by her friends to marry her off to a perfume-store owner. Shortly after coming to California, Pauline learned her acquaintances had received expensive diamonds from the businessman as payment for giving him Pauline's hand in marriage. Pauline got out of having to marry the stranger by claiming she was betrothed to a man from New York who would soon be joining her. In a letter sent back home to her friend in November of 1885, she wrote that she thought "the whole transaction was crazy to go so far" without her knowledge.

African-American women like Pauline Williamson who challenged such practices forged the way for other black women to freely come west and start a life unencumbered by social restrictions. Nevertheless, members of the Busy Bee Club and other like-minded black organizations helped transform the sparse frontier into a thriving, racially diverse country.

Marriage & Money

It is said that early pioneers were compelled to go west. Their strong desire to learn what was beyond the boundaries of the Mississippi River beckoned them. Thousands of men made the initial trek over the plains, many of them unencumbered by a wife or children. It was an isolated and lonely existence for them, but given the fact that there were few single women living on the frontier, there was little they could do about their circumstances.

Women who remained in the East experienced a similar lack. The push to expand the United States territories, the fever of the Gold Rush, and the Civil War claimed the greater majority of marriageable men. The highest percentage of unmarried women in American history was recorded between 1860 and 1880. According to the November 1886 edition of the *Ladies' Home Journal,* the reasons for the decreased male population in the area and for the decline in wedding vows being exchanged went beyond politics or the urge to find wealth. Rather, there was a close connection between marriage and the price of wheat, beef, pork, beans, corn, and other things. "As the prices of these commodities went up the number of marriages went down," the article explained.

The *Ladies' Home Journal* article also supplied the marital statistics they had compiled.

From 1851 to 1854 times were good, food was cheap and people getting married before heading to California's gold fields went up to 25 per 1,000. Between 1855 and 1858 there was a great depression in trade, and in 1858, the marriage rate went down to 17 per 1,000. The years from 1873 to 1879 form another period of depression. Factories were closed and manufacturers of every kind suffered severely. In one year at least, crops were short and the prices of food were high. The result was immediately seen in matrimony, for in 1874 the number of marriages went down from 21 per 1,000 of the population to 18 and in 1878 and the following two years declined to 15 per 1,000.

Almost as unfavorable as that of hard times is the influence of war upon matrimony. During the Civil War the number of marriages in the country fell off from 20 per 1,000 of population to 17 per 1,000 and immediately after the civil war was ended in 1865, the number rose to 22 per 1,000, declining in 1869 to 21. The women who were looking for a husband had a better chance of getting one just before or just after the war than at any other time.

Many single women hoping to find a spouse between 1865 and 1869 attended college. Ambitious women enrolled in schools across the eastern portion of the states were seeking to become doctors, lawyers, and journalists. Unfortunately for these ladies, men viewed female college graduates as poor homemakers, and the few eligible bachelors around kept their distance from educated ladies. Not knowing where else to turn, women who wanted to flee the shame of spinsterhood—as well as men who had settled in a wild land far from home and were in desperate need of companionship—turned to mail-order magazines to find a spouse.

Fascinated by the popularity of mail-order bride ads and other businesses that focused on bringing couples together, the March 15, 1891, edition of the *Salt Lake City Daily Tribune* featured a series of articles on the subject of marriage. In particular, the articles focused heavily on what men and women want and don't want in a mate.

The wedding dress featured on the front page of *Harper's Bazaar* on November 13, 1886, was the most desired gown by mail-order brides of the time.

The author, Barbara Balzac, began one article with an assertion that women could not be expected to give a qualified answer when asked to give their opinion on marriage. "I do not think women are capable for each one is certain to judge from her standpoint and that alone, and so she cannot look at the question in an unprejudiced way."

The first man the columnist interviewed for the paper was a member of a number of civic organizations. He revealed that three-quarters of the men in the clubs with him were married, but they spent a great deal of time away from their wives. In the meantime, the single men around were lonely and desperately prayed for a wife. "If he had one he would never leave her at home to attend a club function," the man shared with the reporter, apparently unaware of the self-contradictory nature of his comment.

The next man to address the subject was a doctor. "A man needs the right sort of woman," he said. "That woman is best described as a combination of the ideal and the material. . . . But how many men find her?"

The next gentleman Balzac spoke with was a bachelor and did not ever want to change his circumstances. "A man and woman get married, expect to be together for 365 days in the year," the bachelor elaborated, "and never take the time to find out whether they are calculated to be happy together. A man has a right to claim in marriage all that friendship would give him and a great deal more."

Author Balzac expanded on her own thoughts about how a bachelorette could best find a husband and keep him. "If women were more wives and less mothers, marriages would never fail. Too often a husband is forgotten after the birth of a child. Women are undoubtedly creatures of habit, and once they drift into that dangerous sea of thoughtfulness they are very apt to let the little bark marked 'husband' drift away and very often cannot be lured back."

The same article revealed the financial reason some single men wouldn't respond to mail-order bride advertisements, no matter how solitary they felt and how few women there were in the western community where they lived. "My income is so moderate I could not support a wife and children. Married that income would have to be divided by two, and within six months marriage would be a failure," responded one bachelor.

It was a general consensus among all the men interviewed that widows make the best wives. Advertisements placed in *Matrimonial News* or the *New Plan Company* catalog by widows garnered quick responses. The thought was that "women who had had one husband had experience in how to be a good wife, practiced restraint, and could make life smoother overall."

Balzac concluded the informative article with her assessment of the wisest marriages.

> *If girls would only learn that there's not much compliment in being man's first love. The man who goes into a garden of flowers and simply takes the first one he meets, doesn't know what he is doing. It may not be sweet; there may be thorns on it, and it may soon fade. The wise man is the one who goes all through the garden, and seeing them all, selects the sweetest and most important of all, the one that will last the longest. To my mind, more marriages would be successes if women were more loving, more affectionate, more considerate, and more patient. The man should have the most brains of the two. I don't want a woman to be a fool, but I think she should be more loving than intellectual, and more gracious than learned.*

Another article on the same subject, which ran side by side with Balzac's, noted that women who advertise for a husband are anxious to marry, but many of their pleas go unanswered because men are afraid of the opposite sex.

Columnist Mrs. Kate Gannett Wells wrote that some men have a fear of women because they've seen how many have entered into professions and earned financial independence. Men perceived them to have no need for a life partner.

> *Many a man will tell you he cannot afford to keep up a home as the young ladies of today desire to live, while the fact is, a dozen young ladies at his acquaintance would be perfectly content to live modestly and quietly, but it's his own ambition that stands in the way. . . . The average girl is not a mercenary, nor does she*

need to shine as a social luminary to be happy. . . . The American girl has intelligence enough to realize how little true happiness there is in life devoted to display.

The research Wells did for the article led her to the conclusion that most mail-order brides were waiting not for a fortune, but for an honest heart worthy of the love they had to offer. "I do not believe the single woman of forty lives, or ever did live (excepting religious enthusiasts), who would not rather be happily married."

As a result of the many interviews Wells conducted with bachelorettes featured in mail-order bride publications, the author determined that most were not content to be single. "Those that are content must be curious beings indeed," Wells concluded.

Annie Stephens & Asa Mercer

The Belle and the Businessman

The SS *Continental* pitched and rolled as it traveled over the rough waters of the Pacific Ocean en route to the northwestern section of the United States. The nearly three dozen women on board were violently ill with seasickness and desperate for the waves to subside. They were either lying on their bunks in their berths or hanging over the railing of the vehicle heaving into the sea. The tormented females were part of a unique group headed west in search of a spouse.

In 1860, Asa Mercer, a twenty-one-year-old educator and entrepreneur, conceived the idea of bringing eligible females to the Washington Territory in hopes of settling the area and making it fit for societal advancements. The Pacific Northwest was known as a man's paradise. Everything a young man ever dreamed of or wanted was there, except young women.

Life without the presence of a woman to share a home and life grew monotonous—so much so, in fact, that a big percentage of single men vowed they would pull up stakes and seek a new place to settle unless someone did something in a hurry. Enter Asa Mercer.

Mercer organized an expedition of prospective brides to go west in 1864. He recruited dozens of young ladies (mostly teachers) to journey to a place where their talent and gender were in high demand. The Mercer Belles, as the primarily Massachusetts-born females became known, welcomed the chance to accompany the businessman on his second voyage to the growing coastal town of Seattle. In addition to offering the chance to meet and marry ambitious, hardworking bachelors, Mercer promised the eager, single passengers honorable employment in schools and good wages.

When the SS *Continental* left the New York harbor on January 16, 1866, there were thirty-four women on board. Each paid a $225 fee for the opportunity. Each possessed high hopes and a sense of purpose. Nevertheless, after traveling one hundred miles in rough, heavy surf, the physically unwell Belles were pleading with Mercer to take them back home. Eventually the waters calmed, and all sea-sickness disappeared. The women then slowly began the process of acclimating themselves to the ship and making themselves at home.

Among the energized female passengers was twenty-six-year-old Annie Elizabeth Stephens, an Irish-Catholic lady from Baltimore. Annie and her sister Marnie, nine years her junior, had been persuaded to join the expedition after hearing Mercer's compelling speech about the wonderful opportunities in the Northwest. He told of the "wonderful financial advantages that would occur to any and all young ladies of good character." According to the bachelor teacher, "Dressmaking offered a great chance to make a lot of money." Annie believed her fortune was far away from the congested eastern city of Lowellton, Massachusetts, where she was raised, and she was more than willing to sign up for the journey Mercer so enthusiastically promoted.

The female passengers, who agreed to take the boat trip from New York through the Strait of Magellan to Seattle, were informed of the difficulties they would face along the way. They were told about the rough waters, unsettled weather, unpredictable temperatures, and cramped living quarters, but it did not change their minds about making the three-month-long voyage. The chance to marry and the idea of continual employment, where four dollars a week payable in gold was assured by Mercer, were worth any risk.

The curious sailors and crew aboard the bride ship were intrigued by the women who participated in Mercer's unique expedition. They were not immune to the desire for female companionship, and for many, keeping their focus on their job was difficult at times. Some of the men were cynical about the idea of female emigration and considered any woman who sailed with them less than honorable. Newspapers such as the January 28, 1866, edition of the *Daily Alta California* reported, "It may be well doubted whether any girl who goes to seek a husband in this manner is worthy to be a decent man's wife, or is ever likely to be."

Annie Stephens was convinced the venture would be beneficial for both herself and her sister. Born in Philadelphia on January 4, 1840, to the owner of a hat factory and his wife, Annie was an independent thinker. She believed women should pursue higher education and assert themselves politically when necessary. Annie was considered by some members of the SS *Continental* crew to be a bigot who possessed a superior attitude because of her religion. She was outspoken and brash—and she had set her sights on the unwitting Mercer shortly after the ship had set sail.

Asa Shinn Mercer was born on June 6, 1839, in Princeton, Illinois. He was the youngest of thirteen children. He claimed that he had spent a great deal of time with Abraham Lincoln when he was a boy and that Lincoln had been a major influence in his life. He credited Lincoln with encouraging him to travel. Mercer made his first trip west in 1852 and eventually helped settle the Seattle area with his brother Thomas. Both men scouted the Puget Sound region and established various businesses together, such as a mercantile and lumber mill. Mercer Island in King County, Washington, is named for the Mercer family. Asa returned to the Midwest

IS WASHINGTON TERRITORY IN DANGER?

THE MODERN ARK, THE MODERN NOAH, AND THE MODERN "WATERFALLS" THAT ARE ABOUT TO
DESCEND UPON WASHINGTON TERRITORY.

THE MODERN NOAH (*loq.*). "There, my dear young ladies, I think I see something."
CHORUS OF 400 UNMARRIED WOMEN. "Oh! please, Sir, is it a Man?"
THE MODERN NOAH. "No, bless ye! not a Man; it's a Gull."
MARY ANN (*aside.*) "Oh, dear! I wonder when we'll see a Man!"

On February 3, 1866, *Harper's Weekly* noted the arrival of the latest "Mercer Girls." WASHINGTON STATE HISTORICAL SOCIETY

to attend Franklin College in New Athens, Ohio, in 1860. Once Mercer graduated, he went back to Seattle and helped establish the Territorial University of Washington. He was then hired on as the school's president.

Although Annie and the other Mercer Belles were expected to arrive in the Northwest unattached, that assumption did not stop the crew from flirting with the women and suggesting they marry a sailor rather than a pioneer. Most of the women were flattered by the attention and readily engaged the seamen in conversation. With the exception of Mercer, everyone on board passed the time together playing card games and singing and dancing. As the leader of the expedition, Mercer felt he should resist any involvement with the potential brides. His resolve weakened after spending time with two of the Belles; Annie was one of them.

Prior to the expedition setting off for the Northwest, Mercer told his crew that he was an "incorrigible bachelor," and that no fair lady among the entire party could draw from his heart those exquisite lines of Shakespeare: "Is't possible that on so little acquaintance you should like her? That but seeing you should love her? And loving woo?" Not only did Cupid turn Mercer's thinking around, but also Annie wasn't the first to make his heart swoon. According to the journal of Roger Conant, a crew member with the SS *Continental* who made note of Mercer's comment about being an "incorrigible bachelor," Mercer was initially charmed by an aspiring teacher making the trip "who was of good report and fair to look upon." Try as he might to convince the young woman that he would make a fine husband, she did not agree with his assessment. "Poor deluded young man!" Conant wrote in his memoirs. "He imagined that simply because he was the agent of this expedition that all the virgins were desperately in love with him, and were only waiting for him to offer himself, to fly into his arms."

After the woman Mercer was interested in had spurned his advances a number of times, he had a change of heart and recommitted to life as a bachelor. When Annie captured his affections, he abandoned the notion again. Conant described Annie as a "willing victim, no doubt anxiously waiting for an offer of his [Mercer's] heart and hand."

On July 15, 1866, more than two months after the SS *Continental* had reached Washington Territory, Annie Stephens and Asa Mercer were wed. Rev. Daniel Bagley, Mercer's childhood friend, married the couple at the Methodist Protestant Church in Seattle. The Mercers' stay in the city where they were united didn't last long. Lured by the idea of new, more profitable business ventures, the couple moved to Oregon. Mercer took a job in Astoria with the federal government as a special deputy collector for the customs service. The position was a high-paying one. In addition to his salary, Mercer shared in the funds collected from goods that buyers imported without declaring and paying the property tax.

In mid-1867, the lucrative job led to trouble. Looking to add still more to his pay, Mercer helped smuggle caskets filled with alcohol into the United States from Victoria, British Columbia. When officials found the cache of illegal whiskey and brandy, they seized the beverages, investigated the source behind the shipment, and arrested several corrupt customs workers for their participation in the crime. Mercer was among the accused. The case against him was eventually dismissed because key witnesses were missing, but Mercer's future as a customs agent was over.

By 1873, the Mercers had turned their attention to real estate. Annie purchased two pieces of property in Washington for $840, and her husband bought additional acreage for $2,000. Prior to the smuggling charges, the couple had purchased three hundred lots in Astoria. When real estate failed to satisfy, Mercer entered into numerous business ventures that failed, costing him and his wife the majority of the money they had earned. The Astoria investment eventually provided a significant return, but not in Mercer's lifetime: In 1970, Mercer's ancestors sold the property for a substantial sum.

The Mercers had eight children: six boys and two girls. Three of those children died in infancy, and one died as a teenager. Annie suffered from poor health before and after the birth of their children and frequently traveled to the drier climate of Denver to improve her condition. Exactly what she struggled with was never revealed. Some historians speculate she suffered from tuberculosis.

Asa Mercer relocated his family to Sherman, Texas, in 1875, where he worked for a newspaper called the *Sherman Courier* as a reporter and researcher. He was particularly interested in owning and operating a newspaper of his own because he believed it made settlers better informed and was the perfect platform to share his conservative views on capital punishment. After an eight-year stay in Texas, Mercer moved his clan to Wyoming. He established a newspaper in Cheyenne called the *Northwest Live Stock Journal* with salesman Samuel A. Marney. While waiting for the business to turn a profit, Annie supplemented the family income teaching piano lessons in the community. At their mother's insistence, the Mercer children attended parochial schools in the area.

Annie was a fierce defender of her husband. Critics of the paper and an unruly business partner were no match for her. In the summer of 1884, Mercer and Marney had a heated disagreement in front of Annie. The argument, which started when Mercer fired an employee Marney favored, became physical, and Marney beat Mercer unconscious. Annie interceded at that point and hit the man on the head with a spittoon, knocking him out. Apparently Marney and Mercer worked out their differences in a more civil manner, because for a short time Mercer continued working for the paper as a reporter.

In 1895, Asa and Annie left Cheyenne and moved to Paint-rock Valley in northern Wyoming. Asa and his two sons developed a farm and cattle ranch in the Big Horn Basin that was several thousands of acres in size.

Annie Mercer died on October 16, 1900, at the age of sixty. Asa passed away in 1917 after a prolonged bout with chronic dysentery. He was seventy-eight years old. He never remarried after losing Annie. The Mercers were married for thirty-four years.

Making Matrimony Pay

Long after an advertisement is placed in the newspaper by lonely hearts in need of a spouse, and once nerves have settled after meeting the bride or groom of choice for the first time, comes the challenge of making a mail-order marriage last. Matches that came about through a public announcement, marriage broker, or matrimonial agency in the mid-1800s were not necessarily unhappy. Though embodying more of the lottery element than the ordinary marriage is said to contain, they frequently yielded surprises to the persons involved.

Conscientious marriage brokers like Edgar Kaborchev of Bachmut, Russia, wanted his clients to be satisfied with their decision for a lifetime. Kaborchev resided in New York City and represented several men west of the Mississippi looking for a bride. According to the June 23, 1890, edition of the Logansport, Indiana, newspaper the *Daily Reporter,* Kaborchev provided photographs of those interested in marrying so "the individual who hired him could make a more informed decision about the persons entering into such a sacred union." Each photograph was accompanied by details concerning the social and financial standing of the person pictured.

The *Daily Reporter* noted that Kaborchev was "kindly received everywhere." He was quick to point out to the eager men and women he had arranged to marry that he wanted them to be happy for years. "Knowing a potential spouse is attractive and of fair fortune before they exchange vows is the key to success," Kaborchev proudly confessed.

It won't be my fault if I die an Old Maid

My mother pretends for a wife I'm too young,
and says that men will deceive me.
But let her look back, she'll soon hold her tongue;
if not, 'tis no matter, believe me.
Sweet gentlemen, don't be a moment in fear,
and suffer a damsel to keep singing here,
remember a thought to no girl is so dread,
as the terrible one–that she may die an old maid.

Mother preaches forever against men, the vile sex,
and says every look is alarming,
but, between you and I, this she says only to vex,
for I know that she thinks you all charming.
Three husbands she has had in the course of her life,
now I only want one, sir, "Pray who'll have a good wife?"
Now men don't be stupid and look half-afraid!
Speak boldly, or else I must die an old maid.

Men boast they are kind, and easily had,
and lovers are willing and plenty,
I vow it is false, for I've not got a lad,
although I'm turned one-and-twenty.
The man I love best now stands in full view–
don't look so sharp, sir! I did not mean you,
but that handsome man there–O, what have I said,
but it won't be my fault if I die an old maid.

This song was a reaction to the pressure women felt to find a husband. It was initially a poem written in the late 1800s and became a popular song in the early 1920s.

This advertisement for the Halcyon Matrimonial Company ran in *The New York Times* in 1898.

On the other hand, many marriage brokers did not extend themselves beyond locating people who simply wanted a husband or wife. They did not bother to take into account their clients' specific needs or desires. Such was the case of an Iowa woman who hired a broker in October 1886. When she met the man from Oregon that she was engaged to marry in Independence, Missouri, she was shocked to find he was missing an eye. "A devise of glass occupied the absent organ," the New York paper the *Syracuse Standard* reported on December 11, 1886. The young woman considered calling off the engagement, but her fiancé managed to convince her he would make a fine husband, and the ceremony was performed. "Perhaps she reflected that love, himself, is blindfolded," the *Syracuse Standard* article read, "and may as well have crystal orbs as any other; or suspected that the bandage he wears is only the cocoon of a pair of glasses."

In the mid-1890s, marriage brokers were charging $200 to $750 to match each client with a suitable spouse. The negotiated price was usually paid once the couple wed, and the broker witnessed the union. Occasionally, clients would avoid payment by eloping. Otto Fredrich Oskar did just that—but without his betrothed—in July 1897.

Earlier in the year, Oskar had hired Emma Thumann to locate a suitable wife for him. Emma arranged for the German baron to walk down the aisle with thirty-year-old widow Margaretha Braut. The widow's late husband had been a butcher who died of heart failure in 1894. He left her nearly $75,000 when he passed. Oskar was a widower in search of a bride who possessed not less than $20,000.

Shortly after the pair were introduced, a wedding date was set. Oskar visited with Margaretha, her parents, and younger sister, Barbara, at their home in Nebraska. All agreed he would make an exceptional husband. Margaretha's sister took an instant liking to Oskar, and he was equally enamored of her. Margaretha was so focused on the upcoming nuptials that she didn't notice Barbara and Oskar exchanging flirtatious glances. Before Oskar left his fiancée's home after having made her family's acquaintance, he borrowed $500 from her to prepare for their New York honeymoon.

When Oskar did not return the following day and Margaretha's sister was gone along with all her clothes and personal belongings, the bride-to-be thought the coincidence was too much not to be believed. Overnight Oskar and Barbara had fled to New York and were married by a justice of the peace. Margaretha was furious, as was Emma Thumann, who hadn't been paid for her services. The angry jilted bride notified the police, demanding Oskar be arrested for having secured money under false pretenses. Emma pressed charges as well for unpaid fees.

The couple eluded pursuit and spent the funds Oskar had acquired from Margaretha on general extravagances, clothing, and presents for one another. Once the pair ran out of money, Oskar went in search of a job and found a position as a waiter in a concert saloon in Hoboken, New Jersey. Dressed in a long white apron and answering to the name of Fritz, Oskar passed from table to table carrying drinks, while girls danced to the rhythm of a four-piece band on a small stage.

When the authorities finally caught up to Oskar, he denied he'd received any money from Margaretha, but after a quick interrogation, he finally confessed to taking a much lesser amount than was claimed. The July 17, 1897, edition of the *Boston Daily Globe* reported that Margaretha and Emma wanted Oskar shipped to Munich, where he was originally from, and imprisoned there. "They cannot talk police to me," Oskar announced to law enforcement, "for even if I borrowed money they could not take me back to Munich." The officers agreed with Oskar and explained to the angry women that the offense of getting money under false pretenses was not extraditable.

In addition to printing warnings to mail-order brides and grooms about being on guard for potential mates who might misrepresent themselves, some newspapers relayed information meant to safeguard the less-traveled readers from making cultural mistakes with men or women who responded to their ads from foreign countries. The *Daily Republican* in Decatur, Illinois, carried articles about various courting and wedding customs around the globe. One article in particular, entitled "The Science of Wooing," outlined what was expected of marriage brokers in different lands. "Marriage among some people from different lands is purely a business transaction," the October 29, 1895, article noted. "The natives of southern Siberia, for instance, buy their wives from the parents, paying them sums ranging from twenty to seventy-five dollars according to the attractiveness of the girls. Among the Tartars, the same custom prevails, but the brides are more valuable, some commanding as much as one thousand dollars."

The article continued with vivid illustrations of other far-off nuptials.

A wedding in Korea is described as a unique ceremony. The groom, clothed in a gorgeous gown hired for the occasion, is preceded by his best man who carries a goose in his arms. The procession marches toward a small table before which the groom bows profoundly. . . . Soon afterwards, the bride, chaperoned by two elderly females, makes her appearance. Her face is painted white with ghastly red spots on her forehead, each cheek, and on the lips. Her eyes are sealed. She is led across a large mat (representing fidelity) in the center of the room. At this moment, the bridegroom is supposed to appear on the other end of the mat. They are both fed by the elderly women, and the seal is then removed from the woman's eyes. They are now married. . . .

In Burma, the lovesick man follows his intended around for three days at a respectful distance. If she decides he is the one she would like to marry, she will turn and smile at him on the third day. At that point, the potential groom can begin wooing in earnest.

The most nonchalant method of courting is practiced in some Australian tribes. When a man happens to see a woman who pleases his fancy he knocks her down with a club and carries her to his hut. Among the Bengals of India, the woman does the chasing.

In Russia, the bride is conducted to the church by two young men and the groom by two bridesmaids. After the marriage ceremony, the bride is conducted to her new home by the relatives of her husband, and the groom is placed in charge of his wife's people.

The last cultural example provided in the article reflected the writer's decidedly elevated view of a European tradition.

An important factor in comparatively recent development in all matrimonial negotiations is the marriage broker. People in this profession have existed in some fashion since time immortal. In parts of Asia and Eastern Europe, they have always been considered important personages; but in genteel society, they were not recognized until very recently. The marriage broker in Paris is the Prince of his profession. He usually maintains a proper establishment on one of the main boulevards. Applicants for either husbands or wives schedule a meeting with the broker. After an applicant and his wants have been entered into the books, the agent then hires sub-agents who are aware of all the financial circumstances of the wealthy families. These designate a man or woman, as the case may be, whose social position corresponds with the requirements of the applicant. The agent next ascertains what places of public amusement are frequented by the person he wants to meet. Having accomplished this he makes use of the large circle of acquaintances in all classes of society and secures an introduction. It is then a very easy matter to bring the two people together and in nine cases out of ten marriage results. For his trouble the broker receives an entrance fee and a certain percentage of the bride's dowry.

The *Daily Republican* article concluded with a verse from the book of Proverbs that has been repeated throughout the centuries many times: "Whoso findeth a wife findeth a good thing."

The Bride & the Hoarder

Boards, automotive parts, and motorboat engines blocked the main entrance of a majestic home in Ogden, Utah, known as the White mansion. Nearly every inch of the yard surrounding the house was crowded with engines, windshields, tools, and tires. The interior of the house was in the same condition. It was difficult for residents living near the magnificent estate to imagine how anyone could exist among the overwhelming clutter. The owner of the massive property, Frank E. White, was a wealthy, eccentric businessman who collected anything having to do with motor vehicles. In 1931 he used his hobby to rid himself of a mail-order bride he regretted having married.

According to the October 5, 1931, edition of the Ogden, Utah, newspaper the *Ogden Standard Examiner,* Frank White had been married multiple times after his first wife died giving birth to their first child. He married and divorced four women in quick succession after the tragedy, creating quite the scandal in the process. Few people spoke aloud about the frequency with which White was in and out of marriages. It wasn't until his fifth trip down the aisle that neighbors gave him disapproving glances and whispered among themselves, "Another! What can the man be thinking?"

White met his fifth bride through the Pacific Matrimonial Bureau based in San Francisco, California. Their wooing and cooing began by mail in the fall of 1930. Ava Kurth, a twenty-two-year-old woman from Providence, Rhode Island, married Frank White on November 10, 1930. For a while it seemed Ava and

Frank were happy together. He was even considering reentering local politics. He had abandoned all but a few interests when his first wife passed away. It is reported that under Ava's influence he even took his best Sunday-go-to-meeting clothes out of the mothballs and became for a short period an approximation of the sartorial elegance which had been one of his outstanding characteristics when his first wife was alive.

"Imagine their surprise and chagrin, then, when Mr. White bought several automobiles to add to the numerous automobiles he already owned, attired himself in his oldest rags, and started tinkering with the mechanics of the cars," the report in the *Ogden Standard Examiner* read. "Within a few weeks he had completely dismantled the cars he had acquired, and had scattered the parts about the front lawn of the White abode."

White's interest in things mechanical continued to grow. Day after day, wrecked, decrepit, disreputable-looking automobiles of all kinds were driven or towed onto the estate, and White worked from dawn to dusk dismantling them. Ogden residents were aghast. Among the distinguished inhabitants of the area where White lived was the governor of the state, who drove down White's street for the sole purpose of viewing the debacle.

It became easy to see that all was not right between the distinguished junk-collector and his mail-order bride. Neighbors reported that White and Ava had wordy altercations with one another in their front yard in the middle of the day. They noticed that Ava began to go away for days at a time and that on those occasions White worked even more vigorously on the vehicles, carrying carburetors, radiators, windshields, tires, rims, and steering gears into the mansion and returning empty-handed. According to the same *Ogden Standard Examiner* article, "As soon as the grounds of the place were thoroughly littered with automobile parts, White turned his attention to nautical paraphernalia. He purchased items from estate sales and other collectors. Soon the two magnificent boat-houses that sat on the property were filled to the eaves with dismantled parts."

People didn't know that of the fifteen rooms in the White mansion, fourteen were piled practically to the ceiling with junk. People didn't know that the kitchen alone remained clear of used iron, steel, and rubber. They did notice that Ava put in a permanent disappearance, and many said they did not blame her. They were not the slightest bit surprised when she filed for divorce. "Frank White admitted he did not really love Ava and wanted her to go," the *Ogden Standard Examiner* article continued. "So he filled his fine home with junk to crowd her out. Ava told neighbors the house was not a fit place for anyone to live."

White kept a small cot in the kitchen for himself and spent the last years of his life alone, apparently satisfied with his lot.

Matrimonial News Features

The average edition of the *Matrimonial News* contained much more information than advertisements from people seeking spouses. Readers also could peruse stories of men and women who had found their true love using the paper, advice on what to wear and not to wear, poetry, and even tips on spelling and grammar. The editorial department considered such material "helpful to the unmarried reader searching for agreeable company."

A poem entitled "Love's Garden," by Earl Jervis, first appeared in the March 15, 1888, edition of the *Matrimonial News,* and portions of it were often quoted in ads placed by singles looking for that special someone.

> Love kept a garden: in it there grew
> One little blossom, lowly and true;
> And Love, the gardener, set it apart:
> Cherished it, tended it, christened it "Heart."
> Love wrought a canopy over his flower:
> Fashioned a dark and inscrutable bower—
> Love twined the leaves of it, calling them "Fears,"
> Springing from Hope, and watered by Tears.
> Each day a Sunbeam danced o'er its bed,
> But never a glance for the leaf-hidden head:
> And, oh, Heart was weary when Sunbeam tripped by,
> Till from his cradle he lifted his cry:
> "Sweet little Sun-ray, would it were mine
> To grow where thy golden gleams ever might shine;

So in the lovely night, comforting me,
Moonbeam they photograph ever should be!"
Then Love, the gardener, pruned, in his art,
All that hid Sunbeam from poor little Heart.
"Win they, my blossom, who truthfully woo,
And fair be the bridal of Sunbeam and you!"
With pansies for groomsmen, all velvety bright,
And maidenly snowdrops in vesture of white,
And clear ringing harebells that nodded above,
Heart took him a bride in the garden of Love!

On January 8, 1887, readers were treated to a section devoted to recipes and jokes. Single women serious about acquiring a mate were encouraged to learn to make special dishes that would satisfy a man's palate. The article suggested that "gentlemen enjoy nut cake with tea or coffee, served at an elegantly set table." The recipe for nut cake was as follows: "Three eggs, one & one half cups of sugar, one-half cup of butter, one-half cup of milk, two and one-half cups of flour, one and one-half teaspoons full of baking powder, one cup of the meats of any kind of nuts."

Single men determined to find a "fair or gentle" someone to bring them happiness were encouraged to hone their joke-telling skills. "The finer sex appreciates a sense of humor," the magazine noted. The predominately male editorial staff contributed an epigram to be used at the "right occasion"; it was entitled "Better Than a Door-Bell."

A pair of lead knuckles weighing seven or eight ounces were taken from a prisoner who was being searched at headquarters the other day, and the sergeant picked them up and asked: "What do you use these for?" "To knock on the door and rouse up my wife when I get home late," was the reply. "Then they answer the doorbell, eh?" "That's it, sir, only they are ten times as reliable. You can't hit your wife with a doorbell if she comes downstairs jawing, but you can with those. I'm a poor man, sir, and have to study all sorts of economy."

The headline across one portion of the *Matrimonial News* read FEMININE FASHION TIMELY INFORMATION PRESENTABLE IN A READABLE, CONCENTRATED FORM. The suggestions offered claim to have something for everyone. Here are a few examples:

Yellow is a favorite color for elegant negligee toilets. Frieze cloth is very popular for promenade jackets this season. Plain velvets are more fashionable than brocade for dress wraps. Style and comfort are combined in a large hood made of dark plush lined with satin. Newly imported French bonnets show combinations of velvet and fur of the same shade. The fur is used only on the brim. English and Spanish turbans made entirely of plumage, the crowns covered entirely with fine feathers, are once more popular. Labrador blue is a new color, which will be used in dark and light shades, the former for street, and the latter for evening wear.

A listing of the best honeymoon spots was a well-liked feature in the publication. Couples fortunate enough to marry the individual whose ad they responded to wanted to know the most romantic retreats to celebrate their union. New York, Washington, D.C., and Boston were frequently named ideal destinations, but, in late 1886 into early 1887, a significant number of bridal couples were traveling to the Crescent Hotel and Spa in Eureka Springs, Arkansas.

An article written about the hotel that appeared in the October 22, 1886, edition of the *New York Times* suggested honeymooners travel by train to "America's most luxurious hotel." The Frisco Line, a plush passenger train with palace-style sleepers, transported brides and grooms to Eureka Springs. "The Crescent

The Kansas City edition of the *Matrimonial News* published photographs of prospective grooms like this gentleman.

Hotel and Spa is a year-round resort hotel," the report read. "This famous health and pleasure resort has no equal in the western country. Only fifteen hours from St. Louis and rates cheaper than to any other great resort. For health and pleasure you can not do better than to visit Eureka Springs, Arkansas." Built at a cost of $294,000 in 1886, the Crescent Hotel treated newlyweds to fine cuisine and dance parties, with music provided by an in-house orchestra.

"Washington hostelries are literally filled with blushing brides," the article entitled "Blushing Brides" began. "Washington is becoming more and more a favorite place on the wedding tour. Everything is cheerful, there are enough sights to occupy the time for months, and then the presence of the new partners lends a kind of solace found at no other place."

Although the *Matrimonial News* was not regarded by most in the newspaper industry as a serious journalistic endeavor, it appealed to the mass market. It encouraged lonely individuals to dare to reach out to others and share a bit of themselves for the possibility of the much sought-out happily-ever-after life. Possibly seeking to appeal to a broader market, the paper's editor noted in a weekly column that "at the very least one could gain a friend—if not a husband or wife."

The Murderous Mail-Order Bride

When Carroll B. Rablen, a thirty-four-year-old veteran of World War I from Tuttletown, California, advertised for a bride, he imagined hearing from a woman who longed to spend her life with him hiking and enjoying the historic, scenic beauty of the Gold Country in northern California. The ad he placed in a San Francisco matrimonial paper in June 1928 was answered by Eva Brandon. The thirty-three-year-old Eva was living in Quanah, Texas, when she received a copy of the matrimonial publication.

If Carroll had been less eager to marry, he might have noticed the immature tone Eva's letters possessed. If he'd taken the time to scrutinize her words, he might have been able to recognize a flaw in her thinking. According to the July 14, 1929, edition of the Ogden, Utah, newspaper the *Ogden Standard Examiner,* one of Eva's first correspondences demonstrated that she not only seemed much younger than thirty-three years old but she also had a dark side. "Mr. Rablen, Dear Friend," the letter began. "You wrote about a son I have. He has had no father since he was a month old. The father left me. I haven't seen him. If a man leaves me I don't want to see them. And I'll make sure I can't."

Eva left Texas for California in late April 1929. She and Carroll were married the evening of April 26, 1929. The dance that took place at the Tuttletown schoolhouse on April 29, 1929, was well attended by Carroll's friends and neighbors. They were happy he had found someone to share his life. Eva twirled around the room, dancing with anyone who wanted to join her. She was elated with her situation. Carroll, on the other hand, chose to wait outside in the car for his new bride. According to the *Ogden Standard Examiner,* Carroll was slightly deaf and despondent over the other physical ailments that kept him from fully enjoying the festivities.

When Carroll's father, Stephen Rablen, began regaling guests with his rendition of the song "Turkey in the Straw" on his fiddle, Eva excused herself and went outside to visit with her husband. She took a tray of sandwiches and coffee to him. He smiled proudly at her and commented on how thoughtful it was for her to bring him some refreshments. Carroll helped himself to a cup of coffee, blew across the top of it to cool it down, then took a sip. He made a bit of a face as if the coffee lacked something. He took another drink to determine what it needed.

Shortly after Carroll swallowed the brew a third time, he dropped the cup and began to scream. Eva watched him slump over in the front seat of the car. Carroll continued to scream. Wedding guests poured out of the building to see what was wrong. Carroll's father pushed past the people to get to his son. "Papa. Papa," Carroll repeated, reaching out for Stephen's hand. "The coffee was bitter . . . so bitter."

Emergency services were called to the scene, but by the time they arrived, Carroll had slipped into an unconscious state. Attendees at the reception told reporters for the local newspaper that Eva simply stood back and watched the action play out around her. She wore no expression at all, no worry, concern, anxiety—nothing. An ambulance transported Carroll to the hospital, and Eva rode along quietly in the vehicle with her husband. He was pronounced dead at the scene.

Because Carroll's illness came on so suddenly, doctors suspected foul play. An autopsy was performed, and the contents of Carroll's stomach revealed the presence of poison. The cup he drank coffee out of was also analyzed, and traces of poison were found there as well.

On May 1, 1929, the day of Carroll's funeral, the sheriff of Tuolumne County returned to the spot where the groom had died. In a patch of grass only a short distance from where Rablen's automobile was parked, a bottle of strychnine was found. The bottle was traced to a drugstore in nearby Tuttletown. The register showing the purchase of the item had been signed for by Mrs. Joe Williams. The description of Mrs. Williams given by the clerk at the drugstore suggested Eva Brandon Rablen had bought the item.

The sheriff then asked Carroll's widow to accompany him to the drugstore where, without hesitation, the clerk identified her as the purchaser of the poison.

Authorities escorted Eva to the police station, and she immediately claimed her husband had poisoned himself because he was brokenhearted over his health problems. Stephen arrived at the station soon afterwards and told police that he suspected his daughter-in-law killed his son over a $3,500 insurance policy. He accused Eva of finding her victims through mail-order bride advertisements and suggested she killed her last husband, a mail-order groom named Hubert Brandon. Stephen demanded Eva be arrested for murder.

Eva was arrested for the crime, but not on her father-in-law's orders. A handwriting expert had compared the signature on the drugstore's registry with one Eva provided authorities with at the station. The two were a match. Eva was charged with premeditated murder.

Newspaper articles about the homicide referred to Eva as the "Borgia of the Sierras." The public was ravenous for specifics about the killing. "Quarrels, quarrels, I was sick of and tired of them," Eva told a judge about her marriage. "We talked things over. It was decided we should both commit suicide. But I couldn't bring myself to do it. Finally I decided to poison him. It was the best way out, I thought. Now they want to hang me? I could only put him out of the way because I felt it was the only way to get my freedom."

Eva was sentenced to life in prison at San Quentin for murder. The day the authorities escorted her to the ferry that would take her to the penitentiary she was all smiles. Reporters and inquisitive spectators on hand at the dock asked Eva why she killed Carroll. She politely told them she couldn't give them the information they wanted. "I can't tell you why. I can't tell you why I confessed to putting strychnine in my husband's coffee. I told the court all, and I want to tell all."

Eva was helped onto the ferry that would transport her to San Quentin. Sheriff Jack Dambacher of Sonora County and his wife decided to travel with Eva to prison. "I feel fine," she told her traveling companions, "not a bit tired. I'm not at all downhearted or discouraged." Eva's eleven-year-old son, Albert Lee, waited at the dock with his aunt and uncle to say goodbye to his mother. Eva showed little emotion as she held her child close to her. "I will be all right," she told him. "I'm going to study Spanish. I've always been crazy to learn Spanish. Then if I get along well with that, I can take on other subjects." Eva's sister assured her that she would take very good care of her boy and promised her that those who lived in the Sonora area would help with Albert as well. "He will not suffer for what wasn't his fault. We will see he wants for nothing."

According to the *Examiner*, the 1929 murder of Carroll Rablen by his mail-order bride, Eva Brandon Rablen, is the most notorious case of its type. In addition, the poisoning of Carroll Rablen was one of the earliest cases to prompt scientists to examine potent alkaloids commonly used in homicides and attempted homicides. The study of various poisons—from snakebites to toxic mushrooms—led to the creation of forensic toxicology.

The *New Plan Company* Catalog for Matrimony

Matrimonial clubs date as far back as 1849. Lonely hearts from Syracuse, New York, to San Francisco, California, joined such organizations in hopes of finding a suitable mate with whom to spend the rest of their lives. The New Plan Company based in Kansas City, Missouri, was a matrimonial club that claimed to have more than thirty-two thousand members during its existence from 1911 to 1917. According to the New Plan Company's handbook, printed in the fall of 1910, the plan and method of the club were simple and easy to understand and follow.

> *Our time and money is devoted entirely to the interest of the unmarried. We are dedicated to elevating and promoting the welfare of marriageable people and furnishing them with a safe, reliable, and confidential method at a nominal cost, whereby good honorable people of sincere and moral intentions, may better enable themselves to become acquainted with a large number of such people of the opposite sex as they may deem worthy of consideration, which may lead to their future happiness and prosperity.*

Single individuals who wanted to join the club agreed to pay a five-dollar fee if their membership resulted in matrimony. "Upon the marriage of our member, our fee for our services becomes due," the New Plan Company rules stated. "We aid our members

An unidentified woman in a high-collared dress with lace and ribbons strikes a pose for readers of a mail-order bride publication.   COURTESY, COLORADO HISTORICAL SOCIETY AULTMAN COLLECTION, SCAN #20010214

in every way possible to find their 'ideal' and expect they will be prompt with us when they find the person of their choice."

Club organizers required a one-dollar fee to be paid when hopeful bachelors and bachelorettes applied for membership. That amount would be deducted from the five dollars due and payable at the time they married. "This small fee, which is hardly to be considered as a factor," the *New Plan Company* catalog explained, "keeps away all frauds and curiosity seekers and is a guarantee to us that all persons joining the club are in earnest and not triflers, and this knowledge is certainly beneficial to all members."

Once the initial fee was paid, members received a certificate good for twelve months. For an additional one dollar, members would then be sent a catalog containing the name and address of every man or woman seeking a spouse who had placed an ad with the New Plan Company. "All personal ads in this book are genuine and we have the original letters ordering the insertion of same on file in this office," club organizers assured members. "Most every lady or man whose advertisement we have published has signed a statement in which they agree to answer every letter received from ladies or gentlemen members who enclose postage, either accepting or declining correspondence."

Bachelors and bachelorettes were encouraged to be quick about sending in their application before someone else had an opportunity to engage the attention of the single of their choice. "We believe we are giving you the greatest bargain in the world for your money," the New Plan Company boasted in their literature. "If you know a good thing when you see it, you will lose no time in quickly taking advantage of their most liberal proposition."

Over the course of the six-year period the New Plan Company was in business, the club's staff reported that more than 2,500 single men and women found spouses. According to the 1915 edition of the New Plan Company's handbook, "Most marriages that occurred as a result of an ad placed in the *New Plan Company* catalog were between middle-aged people looking for companionship and security more so than romance."

The following are samples of advertisements placed by singles in the September 1917 edition of the club's catalog.

I do not wish to marry a wealthy man, but one who is comfortably situated and could provide a good home. I am an American; Baptist faith; age, 22; weight, 154; height 5 feet; blue eyes; light brown hair; considered fair looking; occupation, housekeeper. Have means of $2,000 and will inherit $3,000. Respectable, intelligent men only need write.

American; widow by death; age, 38; weight, 135; height, 5 feet 6 inches; brown eyes; brown hair; Methodist religion; occupation, housewife; income $700 per year; business education and musician. Have means of $10,000. I am considered very good looking and neat. Will marry if suited.

My position being such that I have not the opportunity of meeting suitable gentlemen; I take this means of finding my ideal; my age is 38, a maiden lady; weight, 142; height 5 feet 2 inches, brown eyes, brown hair, American; fine housekeeper, neat and plain, and fond of home; would marry if suited.

The people say that I am a good neighbor, a nice housekeeper, good cook and fine manager, always clean and neat, fond of home and children, and try to make home the happiest place on earth; am a widow; American, age 43, weight 120, height 5 feet 4 inches, blue eyes, brown hair, good education; have $500 personal property; object matrimony.

Winsome Miss of 18 years, considered attractive looking, have many friends, very pleasant and lively, blue eyes, dark hair, fair complexion, good education, good cook and housekeeper, weight 130, height 5 feet; would make the right man a good wife; have a profit of $10,000; will answer all letters containing stamps.

An unidentified mail-order couple capture the beginning of their life together in this photograph taken in Oregon in 1866.   CHRIS ENSS COLLECTION

An unidentified woman submitted this photograph for an edition of the mail-order bride publication of the New Plan Company in 1917.

I am a widow of 59 years looking for a companion to travel down life's path with me and make life worth living for; have blue eyes, brown hair, weight 110, height 5 feet; am English descent, a good housekeeper and have small income; I can make the right man happy with a good home.

Here I am boys, all the way from Texas, a black-eyed maiden of 30 years with dark hair, a brunette type, weight 115, height 5 feet 4 inches, nationality German, religion Protestant, college education and piano player; wish to correspond with business men, Western men preferred, between the age of 40 to 45. Will answer all letters.

A nice little blue-eyed Miss from North Carolina, with brown hair, age 18, weight 125, height 54 inches, fair complexion; can sing and play piano; have a fine home, also have means of $50,000; my occupation is trained nurse; would like to hear from a nice young man of suitable age, rich or poor, but must be good-hearted and true; will marry a true love only.

I am a modest little girl of 19 summers with pleasant disposition, black hair, pretty brown eyes, fair complexion, weight 134, height 5 feet 6 inches; I am a farmer's daughter, dress plain but neat; can cook and do housework; American; Catholic; fond of dancing and like amusement; would be willing to live in country; all letters answered. Object, matrimony.

Would like to correspond with a farmer about 30 to 35 years old. Am an American widow of 33; height, 5 feet 2 inches; weight, 200; brown eyes; brown hair; common school education. Personal property worth $1,500. Object matrimony. No flirts need write.

*I am a Virginia widow; have one child, a little boy. I am 28
years old, height 5 feet 5 inches, brown eyes, brown hair; have
$5,000 in town property. Am anxious to meet Western men;
am considered nice looking and by some pretty. Will be pleased
to correspond with Western gentlemen.*

*Am not considered good looking, but make a nice appearance;
plain, and a neat dresser; immaculate character; quiet, loving
disposition; Christian religion, age, 22; weight, 135; height,
5 feet 4 inches; blue eyes; blonde hair; light complexion. Would
like to hear from gentleman interested in missionary work.*

Once a month the editors at the New Plan Company would
publish an article about a specific couple who owed their marital
bliss to the ads placed in their catalog. The August 1913 edition
of the catalog featured the story of friends that lost track of one
another, were reunited through a three-line ad in the *New Plan
Company* catalog and later married.

"An ad in the *News* certainly does pay off," said Mr. J. W. Morgan of Seattle, Washington. It was a little ad in the *"News"* that
helped him find Miss Elizabeth Haans of Des Moines, Iowa, to
whom he was recently married.

*Miss Haans and Mr. Morgan were friends years ago when Mr.
Morgan was an ambitious young teacher in a little Iowa town.
He moved away and as the years passed by the little country
town Miss Haans forgot all about him. She became deeply interested in art and decided to make it her life work. She studied
hard—the best artists of the country were her teachers. About
twelve years ago she came to Des Moines and started a studio.
Someone said she would not last long. The remark reached Miss
Haans' ears. It fired her German and Irish blood (a bad mix-
ture) to antagonize. She said the people would hear from her*

This unidentified, bespeckled subject was one of the many photographs of men presented in the 1917 edition of the New Plan Company's catalog.

before she left Des Moines and she made her word good. She has placed her work as far south as Old Mexico and as far north as Canada and from New York to California. A few years ago her piece of work in the Nude created a regular flurry at the Iowa State Fair. The newspapers carried column after column about it and sent her picture all over the country but not a word was said against Miss Haans.

She saved her money made from her teaching and bought property. She now owns property on the east side. She lived alone for many years. All her friends' efforts to persuade her to marry were in vain and they began to think she was a man hater. She seemed perfectly contented to go life's way alone. What had become of the young schoolmaster? He had married and settled down and became an instructor not only of children but of his own.

Several years ago he lost his wife in an accident. He chose to remain a widower and perhaps would have continued so if he had not by the merest accident learned that Miss Haans was in Des Moines. Until then he did not know where she was. He decided to find her. He had been a member of the New Plan Company for two years. He remembered the New Plan Company catalog had a tremendous reach and hoped beyond hope that if he placed an ad stating he was looking for Miss Haans she might read it.

Miss Haans did not see the advertisement. She was too busy to read the publication. However, many of the daily readers of the catalog saw the ad and one day after she finished a class a friend informed her that someone was looking for her. "Well," said her friend, "you had better answer the ad—it may be a proposal of marriage." "That's so," said Miss Haans. "I never thought of that; I guess I will answer it for I presume that it is the only way I will ever get a man."

Miss Haans did respond to the ad and happily rekindled her friendship with Mr. Morgan. They wrote one another often over a three month period. Five months after the ad was placed in the New Plan Company catalog the couple wed. Mr. Morgan called the New Plan Company office the day after the wedding and thanked editors of the publication for the part the advertisement played in bringing them together.

The staff at the New Plan Company prided themselves on helping their members find their ideal mate and anticipated being paid promptly when the right person was found. "We receive nothing for our time and labor until marriage occurs," the editors assured their members in every handbook published. Members were also assured by the editors that they took their work very seriously. "We realize we have a job to do," the editors noted, "and will work faithfully to fulfill our duties."

Without Any Courting

Among the top stories that made the front page of the June 21, 1873, edition of the *Denton Journal* in Denton, Maryland, were two articles about the *Matrimonial News* publication. The unique periodical was so widely read that some editors felt it necessary to report on its popularity. Under the headline MARRIAGE BY ADVERTISEMENT, journalists noted that the *Matrimonial News* was "the most flourishing property from coast to coast." The writer, however, did not agree it deserved that prosperity. "The editor's confidence in the gullibility and silliness of the public was not misplaced; it is shown in the astounding fact that between three and four hundred sober-minded individuals advertise every week for husbands and wives. One has only to read to be convinced that the advertisements are bona fide and not cooked. . . . But for the evidence furnished by this journal we should not have believed that even ten respective persons would be found weekly."

The reporter investigated the reasons why the *Matrimonial News* was so well thought of by hopeful, unattached men and women. He interviewed many people and came away with the following observations: "A great many ladies are anxious to be a darling to a deserving man and, unable to find someone through traditional mean, believe without reservation the publication can assist them. Of the gentlemen, they are professionals, desperate to marry and convinced the paper would lead the way to a suitable partner."

The *Denton Journal* reprinted a couple of advertisements it felt merited further attention and bore out its theory that those that contribute to the ads are "silly and desperate."

Meckla, well born, sweet-tempered, bright and loving, longs for a tender, soft connubial tie. She values the strong, manful knight of forty, far more than the handsomest, young dandy. So faithful would she be to a noble, pure mind. A more tender heart they could never find.

Marriage – A Nobleman of English birth and ancient Irish lineage, between 59 and 60 years of age, good personal appearance, kind amiable, disposition and sound health, (10 years a widower) is anxious to contract marriage with a lady of about 40, or younger if offered. . . .

The author of the *Denton Journal* article concluded the piece with the same cutting remarks peppered throughout.

What to think of such a newspaper we do not know, but if one-third of the fools who angle for good matches every week in the Matrimonial News *are in earnest, and if one-tenth of them succeed in getting their longing satisfied then we need hardly wonder those who remain single became overweight. No more convincing evidence of the stupendous silliness of human nature was ever offered than this weekly* Promoter of Marriage and Conjugal Felicity. *Signed – An American News Reporter.*

The second of the front-page stories was an example of a man and woman who met via the *Matrimonial News,* married, and lived happily ever after. The article was entitled "Without Any Courting." New York resident Peter Patterson was not a well man; at least, that was his opinion. Among the many ailments he believed he suffered from were headaches, stomach pains, and depression. The pleasant summer that the East Coast city experienced in 1873 did nothing to restore his health or bring about even a modicum of joy. He sought help from his family physician who assured him he was

An unidentified mail-order bride poses for a photograph of the momentous day.

in fine health. "You say nothing ails me, but I can tell what my feelings are better than you can," Peter complained to the doctor. The distraught man speculated he might be suffering from smallpox because he volunteered at a hospital where children dealing with the affliction resided. "I couldn't relish my coffee this morning; left my milk toast untouched," he shared with the doctor. "Hateful life, that at bachelor at a hotel."

The doctor smiled and nodded as if suddenly realizing the reason for his patient's distress. "Why don't you marry then?" asked the doctor.

Peter was taken aback by the doctor's suggestion and informed him that he'd be interested in taking such a step were it not for the extended courting that must precede the commitment: "You spend six months or so, at least, dangling at a woman's apron strings."

The doctor confessed he felt courting was the "fun of it all." His patient turned up his nose and added that there were too few eligible women anyway. The physician then advised Peter to search for a bride in the *Matrimonial News*. The man agreed and after a time found a woman living in Kansas with whom to correspond.

Louise Muntle was a widow who lived on a farm. She claimed to be forty years old, an exceptional cook and seamstress. When Peter learned that she would be willing to take him in for a while, and should he become ill, nurse him back to health, he wrote her right away about meeting. Peter traveled to Kansas, and he and Louise were instantly smitten with each other. Louise later recalled her first thoughts of the suitor. "Nice fellow," she wrote in her journal, "solid, plenty of money; thinks himself ill, but isn't; ought to be married; told him so, but he hates the idea of courting."

Before the first day of their meeting had ended, Peter proposed, and Louise accepted. Louise's grown son and daughter-in-law looked on as a minister performed the marriage ceremony and pronounced the two man and wife.

Louise took good care of her new husband. She fed him home-made bread, fresh strawberries, buttermilk, and herb teas. Peter's complexion was glowing, and his dimples were pronounced. After two short months he was happier and healthier than he'd ever been in his life.

Peter eventually wrote to his good doctor and told him he had taken his prescription, was a married man, and intended to bring his bride back to New York to meet him around Christmas.

The *Denton Journal* wrapped up the positive column with "congratulations to the newlyweds."

"I Do" for a Price

Many individuals were anxious to find a true companion among the list of unattached males and females advertising for a spouse in the various mail-order publications of the mid-1800s to early 1900s. Few women preferred being single, as it meant living a life at or below the poverty level.

In the eighteenth and nineteenth centuries single women were referred to as "spinsters." This derogatory term was used to describe any female between the age of eighteen and thirty who was unmarried and childless—and likely prissy and repressed. The male equivalent of a spinster was a "confirmed bachelor." That term did not carry as much of a negative stigma as "spinster" did, although any such deviations from the accepted and expected social path were met with disapproval.

Regardless of the way society at the time thought of uncoupled women and men, there were those who considered single life a comfortable blessing. According to an article printed in the May 7, 1892, edition of the San Francisco, California, newspaper the *Argonaut*, "[For individuals] without the social standing that a good bank account gives, without being able to keep up with the procession of those who are well dressed, well fed, well situated, and well off, matrimony was out of the question."

The article entitled "They Do Not Marry" explained that unless a person can better themselves materially, there was little incentive to marry at all. "People who have been rich all their lives do not realize what it means to go without luxuries," the article elaborated about the economic conditions of those unmarried men and women living in the East.

But people who have been poor know just the wretchedness of having to wear patched boots and go without lunch; of having to walk long distances, because cab fares "mount up"; of having to refuse nice invitations, because they have no clothes or no means of returning proffered civilities. To these, poverty is a bitter thing, and they loathe it.

Marriage, unless it means escape from carping cares of this kind, they eschew as a hopeless evil. Better endure those trials that we have than fly to others that we know not of, they say. So thinks the everyday, gentlemanly, good looking, entirely personable young man of thirty, who draws an income of from two to four thousand a year, and is asked out all over because he dances admirably and is good to look at and never does anything gauche. So also, thinks the pretty, well bred, well dressed, moderately bright girl of twenty-five, whose father spends six thousand a year and has five children.

Both of these know just the way they want their lives to go. Ever since childhood they have associated with companions who have had more money than they have, and they know how nice it is to be well off. "To be rich or to remain" as we are that is their motto. They do not want to be millionaires, but they do not want to be really pinched financially either. Their house must be large enough and be comfortable. It must be well fitted up—no "sheets by night and tablecloth by day" for them. There must be servants enough to run it. This girl—who has always been comfortably placed, but never luxuriously—has no intention of binding herself down to domestic cares of dusting her own drawing room and turning up hems in her own table linen. Not all that must be done for her. She has made her own dresses and trimmed her own hats all her girlhood, and she wants, when she marries, to change all that. Better to go on doing it in your own home, where it is all you have to worry over, than to do it in your husband's, where you have to keep the house and take care of children as well.

Thus the young lady reasons and rejects her suitors with a peculiar and good humored indifference. She has made up her mind that she will not marry a man who has a cent under five thousand a year, and is not above telling this to the soupirants [a French term meaning "suitor" or "wooer"], who take the hint and strive to realize the ideal. The young lady is quite frank. She is not in the least ashamed of her worldliness or desirous of hiding it under a veil of attractive coyness. She is not mercenary. It is not riches that she demands—comfort that is all: If she is comfortable she will continue to be a very nice, attractive person, but if she has to scrimp and struggle and fight over ten cent pieces, and turn her old clothes, and have her shoes patched, she will not be responsible for her temper. She is a fin de siècle *[meaning of or characteristic of the last part of the nineteenth century, especially with reference to its artistic climate of effete sophistication] to her fingertips— sensible where she might be romantic, practical where she once would have been impassioned—a person who is bound to make a success of her life and keep it on the lines that she regards as the best.*

The young man of her kind holds precisely the same views. Life with a beloved object sounds very charming, but it is not to be indulged in unless the incomes of himself and the beloved object foot up to from five to six thousand per annum. The beloved object on three thousand a year is too expensive a luxury. He cannot afford it. What might have been a courtship dwindles to a mild friendship. Not infrequently he tells the lady of his sad predicament and how impossible a matrimonial alliance it would be on his salary. She condoles with him and they become friends, for no violent fires burn in their hearts and friendship comes quite easily to them.

Marriage would mean a series of sacrifices that neither is willing to make. They would have to live in a flat in Harlem— and no one knows who has not lived in Gotham the horror in which Harlem is held—or a second rate boarding house beyond Fourth Avenue.

Then come clothes and theatres. A New York woman spends money like water on her clothes. She would much rather be well dressed than well fed. She must be well dressed to be up with anything. The moment she grows shabby she is no longer of any importance. Then she may as well give up all the fun and consent to be relegated to dreary insignificance like the old wives of the pashas *[a formal title for military and civil officers, primarily used in Turkey or northern Africa].*

According to an article in the March 15, 1891, edition of the *Salt Lake City Daily Tribune,* one of the other reasons women didn't marry is the issue of health and safety. After reading books written about man's inhumanity to man, some women learned to fear men and marriage. "They are so afraid of being physically mistreated that they have entered professions, and earned financial independence to be free of a reason to marry at all," the article explained. "They feel no need of life partners, whom they might possibly have to support; and they talk with their mothers and find how many lonely moments she has passed in her married life and they dread similar experiences and decide that single life is preferable."

Critics of the *Tribune* article argued that women do indeed marry as frequently as they had in any other period of time and that the percentage of hopeful spinsters is no different than it ever was. "The woman who makes herself satisfied with single life must be a curious being," the critics insisted. "Lungs supply the place of heart in her breast, tepid water the place of blood in her veins. We submit that she does not exist. Let the persistent love, who is even half way her ideal, proved to her that he is dead earnest, and as honest as earnest, and profession and she will welcome marriage like the earth welcomes sunrise."

Edith Collins & William Moore

The Poet and the Texan

When Mary Edith Collins married William Andrew Moore in Willow Springs, Missouri, on October 19, 1913, she had only spent a handful of hours with him. The two were introduced to one another by family friends and courted via mail for several years before William officially proposed on January 27, 1913. He was a twenty-two-year-old farmer from Texas, and she was a seventeen-year-old aspiring teacher. They planned to make a life for themselves in Blessing, Texas. Some of William's family members worked the land in the southeastern corner of the state, and he determined it to be the best possible location for him and his new bride to begin their new life together.

William and Edith (she was not usually referred to as Mary) set off on their journey west on October 22, 1913. It was difficult for Edith to leave behind her friends and family in the small community in the Ozark Mountains. The southern Missouri town of Willow Springs was Edith's birthplace and the only place she had ever lived. She expressed her feelings about the move in a poem she wrote in a journal that had been given to her on March 13, 1910.

Mary Edith Collins COURTESY OF LOIS SMETHERS

William Andrew Moore   COURTESY OF LOIS SMETHERS

I stood at the door step at eve and tide, the wind whispered by with a moan. The fields will be whitening with snow but I will be gone, to roam ore the wild world alone. I stood on the door step when school time was ore, and longed for the time to go by. But now it has gone and I stand here tonight to bid this dear step stone goodbye. Goodbye to my step stone. Goodbye to my home. God bless those I leave with a sigh. I will cherish each memory when I am far away. Goodbye dear old step stone, goodbye. It is hard to be so parted from those that you love when reverses in fortune have come and the strongest of heartstrings are broken in vein. There will be an absence of loved ones at my new home, but I'll abide this poor heartsick soul repeating in vein and brush by each thought of them with a deep heaving sigh. The pain it will cost me no one will ever know, to bid this dear step stone goodbye. There are many temptations which I may meet and sad mournful sights to see every day. But the faces at home, oh I never shall greet their forms for they shall be so far away. But I'll think of the dear old step stone at the door as often drops a tear from my eye. I will stand in my dreams as I stand here alone, to bid this dear step stone goodbye.

Edith's journal was a source of great comfort to her during the trip with her new husband. She poured over the entries with great fondness and recited a few of the items to William. The newlyweds traveled to their first home in a wagon. As William drove the mule team that pulled the vehicle, he eagerly listened to his bride read entries from her diary such as this: "Halloween night. Today I have been picking up potatoes and cutting sprouts. It is just now twenty minutes till 4 o'clock. I am 14 years old. Edith."

Edith was raised on a farm and accustomed to hard work. She felt she was prepared for the challenges of being a farmer's wife. She could plow fields and take care of the livestock and even noted the amount she earned for her labors when she was younger in her journal. "September 19, 1910, Edith Collins worked one day and a half and got .75 cents, worked three quarters of another day and got .80 cents – working cutting meat, working two plowing, $2.00 one half day."

Edith and her four brothers and sister learned their work ethic from their father. He was dedicated to making sure his family was well cared for. In one of the final entries Edith made in her diary before she left home, she wrote about one of the jobs her father did to put food on the table. "This is March the 13, 1913. It is afful muddy today. Papa went to town this morning with a load full of wood he chopped – got $150 for it."

When the wagon train William and Edith were a part of stopped for the evening, Edith would prepare a meal. She made exceptionally good sourdough biscuits and, when it was available, fried okra. She cooked stew in the one good pot the couple owned. Early in their trip the pot sprung a leak, and, due to the lack of funds, it was not replaced until they reached their final destination.

William was anxious to introduce his Texas family to his blushing bride. According to the letters he received from his relatives, they were just as excited about meeting Edith. Prior to reaching Blessing, the pair made several extended stops along the way. The team that pulled the wagon twelve miles a day needed to be rested, the laundry and mending had to be done, and William needed to hunt for their food. Edith's pleasant personality helped her to make fast friends wherever the pair stayed overnight. In Elmore City, Oklahoma, Edith met a fellow traveler named Ethel Harris. Ethel signed Edith's journal and added a verse to convey her sentiments: "Remember me and bear in mind a kind true friend is hard to find. So when you find one just and true, change not the old one for the new."

While William drove the horses and wagon during the day, Elizabeth passed the time making notes in her journal. One of those notes contained information about a man named Jesse James.

In one entry she listed James's birthday as December 12, 1896. In another she noted James had come to meet a relative of hers on March 1913. Prior to learning that the outlaw Jesse James lived from 1837 to 1882, Edith had contemplated the man to have been the same famous renegade from her home state.

Edith and William made it to Texas in early 1914. After a short time working the land with his family, William decided to move to Oklahoma. From there the couple pressed on to Omaha, where they decided to make a living on the Nebraska waterways. Edith and William traveled up and down the North Platte River working as fishermen. Four children later, the pair was still earning their living fishing, but they decided to continue in that line of business on the White River in Arkansas.

By 1929, the Moore family was working the Saint Francis River in Arkansas. Times were hard, and the Great Depression loomed in their near future. William and his sons made twelve dollars a month selling mussels as well as the mussel shells that were used to make buttons. Edith was able to acquire her first pair of glasses from funds earned selling shells.

To supplement the family's income through the 1930s, William, Edith, and their children chopped cotton and picked peaches, grapes, and apricots. When wild game was available, they hunted for their meals. Edith was an expert at skinning and dressing the food provided for her family. She was an exceptional cook as well. Some days she made as many as four dozen sourdough biscuits to feed her hungry brood. Edith's resourcefulness extended beyond the kitchen, too. She made clothing for her children out of flour sacks and sewed quilts for their beds with scraps of material.

Although William and Edith grew to love one another greatly, they were careful never to display their affections publicly. They didn't think it was proper. They shared a passion for the occasional glass of whiskey, reading, and chewing tobacco. Edith recorded in her journal a note William wrote about his wife and one of their common interests: "Tis so sweet to kiss, but oh how better to kiss my sweet – William to the young tobacco-spitter Edith."

Years of hard, nonstop work contributed to William's death by heart attack at the age of sixty-five in 1957. Edith passed away in September 1986. She was ninety-one years old. The Moores were married for forty-four years. The most repeated entry in Edith's journal was a verse written by her friend Ella Cox in Willow Springs before she left on her venture with William in 1913. It seemed to best describe how Edith felt about her self-sacrificing, labor-minded husband: "A handsome husband is hard to find but when you find one true and gay, hold onto his coattails night and day."

The Business of Marriage

Living in loneliness on the plains or in the mountains of the West without female friends on hand, except for the occasional traveler—who may or may not be inclined to be social—the solitary male exile was completely cut off from the companionship of a woman. These lonely souls, who represented a mass of marriageable men, wanted opportunities to cultivate acquaintances. Two of three alternatives available to them were to place an advertisement in newspapers explaining their condition and requesting a wife or to respond to an article from a young woman seeking a husband. Unfortunately not every advertisement was reputable. Opportunistic individuals took advantage of desperate ladies and gentlemen earnestly hoping to find a partner. Such was the case with an advertisement in the June 22, 1890, edition of the *Salt Lake City Daily Tribune.* According to an article about the misleading ad, a couple hundred men were scammed out of money when they answered a woman's plea for a spouse. The third avenue to the altar was through a professional matrimonial agent.

As early as 1846, the marriage broker industry has thrived in the endeavor to introduce men and women from different parts of the United States to each other for the purposes of matrimony. The marriage broker was the Gentile edition of the ancient official Jewish *shadchan* (Hebrew for "matchmaker"), who suggested to parents an eligible man or maid, obtained authoritative information on the important subject of dowries, and conducted the preliminary overtures.

Businesses pursuing this line of work were once referred to as mail-order bride agencies. However, the owners and matchmakers of the various companies abandoned the term in 1910 because they felt it was derogatory. By the early twentieth century the term seemed to imply that women were denied the chance to decide what men they would meet and marry. Reputable marriage brokers prided themselves on full disclosure of both parties' backgrounds and future endeavors.

In 1905, highly successful and honest brokers engineered 2,500 marriages a year. The average price for their services was 2.5 percent of the total net worth of the husband, and they also demanded a fee from the ladies, as well. According to research done by reporters at the *Washington Post* in 1920, more than 60 percent of the marriages arranged from 1848 to 1899 were successful.

The newspaper cited an example of a happy union forged in 1899. A naval officer's daughter, finding herself single at the age of forty-three, threw conventionality to the wind and became the client of a well-respected marriage broker. The article noted that "a gentle woman by birth and education, with no special claim to good looks, and only a small income, met, under the wing of the matrimonial go-between, a middle-aged stock broker, a widower with an income of $500 a year. The marriage broker made all the necessary inquiries, and the couple decided to marry, with the very happiest results."

"Though marriage brokering was sometime open to grave injury and abuses," the reporter for the *Washington Post* noted in the October 15, 1920, edition, "the very fact of its existence and the enormous number of clients was recognition that marriage brokers served a real social want. The necessity is the same everywhere." In parts of the United States in the late 1880s, particularly on the Eastern Seaboard, where there was still a social life, including a continual round of garden parties in the summer and dances at home in the winter, there was an excellent chance to meet a potential spouse. For many beyond the plains, however, there was no opportunity to make that certain someone's acquaintance.

One out of every four matches ended badly. Potential brides and grooms blamed the marriage broker for botched unions. Some felt that the brokers failed to fully disclose their intended's background. The money the brokers received for acting as a link between parties was not refundable. For those men and women who changed their minds about marrying the person to whom they had been introduced—either because they found the broker misrepresented their client's character or the client turned out to have already been married—the matter could be brought before the Match Making Magistrate. The mediation-style court system was funded primarily by brokers across the country. The magistrate listened to arguments from all parties and eventually gave couples the choice to avoid a breach of contract by either marrying then and there or waiting a month to get to know their intended a little better.

In March 1887 a couple in Independence, Missouri, did decide to wait the suggested time before getting married. The would-be groom was the first to voice his reservation. During the crucial waiting period the bride changed her mind about getting married when her intended turned out to be a scoundrel. The woman in the case had contracted the marriage broker to secure a husband. She was plain, in her late forties, and weighed more than 230 pounds. She was willing to pay both the broker $1,000 for a spouse and the suitor $3,000 on the day of their wedding. According to an article in the March 16, 1887, edition of the *Indian Journal*, the man reconsidered the agreement once he saw that she had a "plump figure." He did not tell her his feelings right away. First he convinced the woman to let him have the money to settle a few debts before they met at the altar. The man never showed. The woman endeavored to get her money back but ultimately failed.

In spite of such disappointing episodes, marriage brokers and editors of publications designed for people seeking spouses defended their work to quibblers who claimed their occupation was "cold and unfeeling." "There is nothing really sordid in the frank recognition of the fact that marriages contracted in this matter-of-fact way are, in their genesis founded, on some extent, business like relations," a profitable marriage broker shared with the *Washington Post* newspaper in 1920. "Not sentiment alone, but the great natural law of give and take, is at the basis of the marriage relationship," the broker explained, "and once this is admitted, the proposition to establish matrimonial bureau, social marriage clubs, where millions can meet in social intercourse, will be regarded as a wise and necessary stop."

Many forlorn farmers and cowboys agreed with the assessment that marriage was in part a business arrangement. They depended on matrimonial bureaus and magazines for a wife in much the same way as they did the mail-order houses for their winter underwear. The *Hand and Heart* magazine began as a collection of advertisements from women in search of a companion. Eager bachelors pored over the volume in an effort to find the perfect woman.

Published in London in 1888, the blue linen–covered magazine had an initial circulation of 230,000 and cost readers a penny. Featured along with the mail-order bride ads were articles about how to be the perfect homemaker and mother, the importance of memorizing Scripture, and remembering the Sabbath. Editors of *Hand and Heart* boasted that "its pages had something for the young as well as old readers."

The most popular issue was the bridal volume. Resplendent in a white, red, and gold cover, it highlighted one particular woman looking for a spouse. She was known as the "bride elect." The special edition also included a list of elegant and useful gifts to bestow upon the young lady should she be so lucky as to receive a proposal and get married. The bridal volume also contained an assortment

Marriage Broker: "Here is the lady's picture, she has $30,000. It's a great opportunity for you!"
Wife Hunter (frightened at her face): "I hope to goodness that the picture doesn't flatter her!"

Critics of marriage and brokers of mail-order publications enjoyed making fun of the industry, as shown by this cartoon found in the April 16, 1899 edition of the *Decatur Review.* REPRINTED FROM MICROFILM OF THE *DECATUR REVIEW,* COURTESY OF THE DECATUR PUBLIC LIBRARY, DECATUR, IL of bachelorettes desiring to leave the single life behind. The following are two from more than two hundred advertisements that graced the pages of the American version of the publication.

H&H #242 – We are three jolly and lively girls, all of the brunette order, having dark brown hair and dark eyes, we are all the same age and are quite good friends, 29 years old, of good form: would like to marry three friends or three brothers – we don't want to be too far apart: want correspondence with gentlemen fond of riding horses and attending the theatre.

H&H #234 – A gentlemen of the brunette type, 29 years of age, 5 feet 10, of good character, and earning enough to support a wife comfortably, would like to correspond with a cultured young lady, with a view to matrimony. References exchanged if desired.

Hand and Heart continued to be a well-read journal into the middle of the twentieth century. Couples who owed their marital bliss to the magazine were written about in newspapers across the country. The *Logansport Pharos* newspaper in Logansport, Indiana, carried an article in the October 2, 1903, edition about a bride and bridegroom who met by mail. "Thomas L. Linton, seventy-seven years old, and Mrs. Cynthia A. Alford, fifty-three years old, whose homes are at widely separate points, met by appointment in the Fayetteville County Clerk's office, secured a license, and were married. When they met at the clerk's office, it was the first time they had met in person. Their courtship was conducted entirely through mail after becoming acquainted through a mail-order advertisement."

A similar story made the papers in Biddeford, Maine. According to the March 26, 1916, edition of the town newspaper, Winfred Wohlscleged of Pimo, Idaho, and his bride, Mary Marshal, were on their honeymoon following their marriage in Maine as the result of a matrimonial advertisement romance. Miss Marshal answered a query to her advertisement in the *Hand and Heart* magazine from a man who shared with her that he was a prosperous young fruit grower from Idaho who wanted to marry. They began to correspond, and soon Wohlscleged popped the question by mail.

As the twentieth century embraced progress and change, so did the mail-order bride business. By 1921, picture brides had become the rage. Men and women (mostly women from foreign countries wanting to come to the West) shopped for a spouse using a catalog that contained only photographs of the prospective husband and wife. Readers interested in the looks of one another exchanged pictures. This eventually led to an invitation of marriage.

The first picture bride in history was Mrs. Tomikawa, who arrived in San Francisco from Japan in 1904. She was soon followed by Mrs. K. Ishtomaro in 1905. By 1925, more than eight thousand picture brides had traveled from ports around the world to San Francisco to meet their fiancés for the first time and marry. The women were greeted at the boat by their soon-to-be grooms, clutching the pictures they had been given of their future brides. The women held the picture of their intended high over their heads, and the men searched the photos until they found their own.

Some Protestant churches in the West and women's society clubs criticized the use of matrimonial agencies and, in particular, picture brides. They argued that the practice was dangerous and suggested that naive men and women "opened themselves up to be robbed of all their worldly possessions and money." In Portsmouth, Ohio, a *Portsmouth Daily Times* newspaper columnist disagreed. In an article dated April 5, 1921, Frederic J. Haskin wrote, "The fact is that picture marriages are probably as safe and quite as romantic as any other kind. The peasant girl of Europe is accustomed to the idea of marrying a man she does not know, because over there the parent arranged marriage is the conventional thing."

Referring to what he saw as "an invasion of picture brides," Haskin noted that

to most of us choosing a mate by photograph would seem even more hazardous than most methods, but in all the crowd of picture brides and grooms there were only a few instances of disappointment. The very pretty English girl who had left an Italian villa where she was employed as a governess, to marry a man from Colorado, decided that she couldn't go through with the arrangement when she saw her perspective mate. "I feel that I should marry you, sir, you've paid for my passage . . . but I simply cannot," she told him. "You look very nice and kind, but I am sure we would not get along. Your letters sounded different somehow."

Another girl who was not disposed to accept kindly the husband fate had awarded her was not so polite. She was a large, buxom Syrian lass, with a pair of fine brown eyes that sparkled with excitement when she talked. "I will not marry you," she declared contemptuously as she took in the grotesque appearance of the small built and somewhat elderly gentlemen who claimed her as his property. "You are not the same as your picture – no hair, perhaps no teeth – and you dare to think you can marry me?"

Whether a couple came together by means of an advertisement, a matrimonial broker, or a photograph, many men and women had productive relationships that lasted decades. Their success rate helped make the business of marriage profitable.

Buying for the Bride

On June 5, 1871, twenty-four-year-old Sara Baines, from Louisiana, married forty-eight-year-old Jay Hemsley, of Ohio, at Fort Bridger, Wyoming. Jay had responded to an advertisement placed in the October 12, 1869, edition of *Frank Leslie's Illustrated Weekly*. The two had corresponded for more than a year before Jay, a businessman and farmer, proposed to Sara, a seamstress. A day after meeting at the fort's trading post, the couple was wed.

On his wedding day, nearly two years had passed since Jay read in the August 7, 1869, edition of *Frank Leslie's Illustrated Weekly* about the great need for single women west of Independence, Missouri. "They are badly off for unmarried women 'out West,'" the article stressed. "At Sioux City, Iowa, fifteen hundred of them are wanted immediately to serve in the double capacity of 'wives and mothers.'"

Jay and Sara's wedding ceremony was planned by a few of the excited groom's friends. They decorated low-hanging tree branches along the edge of the Green River, where the couple were to be married, with flowers. Six mismatched chairs pulled from the beds of wagons belonging to generous pioneers were arranged in front of the makeshift altar area. Clear water from the river flowed swiftly past the stand of trees. The grass on both sides of the river was speckled with blooming Indian paintbrush.

Dressed in a gray taffeta dress with black silk bows lining the bustle and sleeves, carrying a bouquet made of wildflowers, the nervous mail-order bride took her place beside the gentleman who would soon be her husband. The fort's minister married the couple.

After they were pronounced man and wife, a photo was taken of the pair.

Mr. and Mrs. Jay Hemsley settled in the area around Placerville, California, where they owned and operated a general store. Some of the items offered for sale at Hemsley Mercantile included merchandise for would-be brides.

Early on, many weddings in the West were simple affairs held at a wagon-train stop en route to Oregon or California. A few nuptials were performed at family homes where only a limited number of guests could be accommodated. According to the December 10, 1908, edition of *Harper's Weekly* magazine, less than 3 percent of mail-order bride weddings were held at churches.

By late 1880, weddings on the wild frontier had evolved into a more recognizably modern celebration and included a lavish cake, dinner reception, elaborate flower decorations, and elegantly dressed bridesmaids and groomsmen. As the turn of the century approached, weddings became extravagant, and stores began designating large sections of their retail space for brides, mail-order or otherwise.

Among the stores in the rugged West that offered merchandise devoted to brides was C. S. Morey Mercantile Company in Denver, Colorado. In November 1902, store executives sponsored a series of articles specifically geared toward women planning their weddings. Entitled "The Bride's Attire," one article noted that "more latitude is allowed when making arrangements for that special day." In the accompanying advertisement, the owners of C. S. Morey Mercantile promised shoppers "pretty and fashionable examples of gowning for the bride and bridesmaids, the 'Going Away' costume and other items for the nuptial season."

According to the November 11, 1904, edition of the Denver, Colorado newspaper the *Evening Post*, "A bride is not restricted to a conventional white satin gown, but has a choice of anything between the most costly and very expensive fabrics. Nor is ivory

Mr. and Mrs. Jay A. Hemsley   CHRIS ENSS COLLECTION

white the only admissible shade, cream white having just now much favor. It makes up prettily and has not that stiff appearance that dead white gives. Lyons satin is often chosen by those who are ultra-fashionable and who can afford to trim the material with the handsome real laces it should have. Old-fashioned grosgrain silks are being used too, as well as soft finished taffeta and embroidered chiffon."

In the early 1800s, it wasn't uncommon for wedding gowns to be made entirely of black taffeta. The gowns could then be used for funerals as well. "Such practices are no longer necessary," the article in the November 27, 1904, edition of the Delphos, Ohio, newspaper the *Delphos Daily Herald* explained.

Trains are different now too. They are very long and cut long at the bottom. An elaborate dust ruffle of chiffon or mousse line is the only trimming for trains of heavier material.

Bridesmaids' gowns are fluffy and airy. While white is the prevailing tint for them, delicate shades are used as well. The bridesmaids' gown may be high-necked or cut out slightly, and have elbow or full-length sleeves, as suits the wearer. Nearly all have corsage ornaments of some kind, a new sort being tinted ribbon roses caught together with twisted folds of ribbon and sprinkled here and there with small artificial velvet leaves.

Next in importance to the wedding attire is the going-away gown. It may be a mix of materials of plain clothes, made with cost en suite. The best design scheme includes light tan broadcloth on its material, self-trimming outlined with black and white silk braid and a tucked white chiffon yoke appliquéd with ecru lace medallions.

In addition to examples of wedding gowns, bridesmaids' wear, and honeymoon garments, the *Evening Post* article also included items a bride "must have" in her trousseau. "A dressy cloth gown with elaborate trimming coupled with a velvet robe is essential. Make it a white broadcloth garment with cream lace and light green velvet belt. Following all these wardrobe suggestions will make you a most stylish bride."

In the May 31, 1916, edition of the *Indianapolis Star,* prospective brides were treated to a full-page announcement of essentials for the wedding ceremony, honeymoon, and life thereafter. Entitled "Shopping with the June Bride," the advertisement recommended ladies consider adding a strand of pearls, a set of luggage, and his-and-hers rocking chairs to her list of keepsakes. Other items included in the advertisement were Oriental rugs, rosebushes, and shoes.

"Knowing that she will need footwear for every occasion, and for this reason, wanting a large and complete stock from which to choose," the ad read, "the bride-to-be goes to the Sample Shoe Store in downtown Richmond, Illinois, for the dainty white satin wedding slippers, the dark serviceable oxfords for street wear, the white kid oxfords for light frocks, shoes for sports wear, comfortable, yet shapely and pretty boudoir slippers, and all other shoes she may need, at standard prices. She buys all of these at the same time without being tired, because she deals with a salesman who is as expert at fitting shoes as he is at selling them."

According to information provided by the staff at the Library of Congress Business Reference Service, many of the traditions followed by brides on the western plains, such as having a photograph taken of the memorable day, were also promoted in newspapers on a grand scale. Weddings, marriage, and life on the western frontier were linked to the American dream. Mail-order couples like Jay and Sara Hemsley realized that dream. The Hemsleys were married for more than fifty-one years.

The Shifty Matrimonial Agent

On February 23, 1891, readers of the *Daily Tribune* in Salt Lake City, Utah, pored over an article about a desperate, young English woman who dreamed of nothing more than being a wife. At twenty-one years of age, Gladys Knowles feared she would die an old maid. Most of her friends had married, but she had yet to meet a man who could hold her interest for more than a few dates. Dressed in a champagne-colored dress outlined in frills of French lace, and with a hat to match, Gladys walked to the *Matrimonial News* office in the Strand district of London. An advertisement for a spouse was tucked inside her drawstring bag. She hoped the notice would bring a quick resolution to her dilemma.

Leslie Fraser Duncan, founder and editor of the unique journal, proudly referred to himself as a marriage broker. He opened the first matrimonial agency in England in 1870. A weekly newspaper sprang from the success of the venture, and similar publications were duplicated in the United States. The sixty-three-year-old entrepreneur claimed to have helped thousands find their soul mates.

A correspondent for the London newspaper *Pall Mall Gazette* described Duncan as a "competent looking man with a thick, drooping mustache and long, gray beard. The top of his head was bald, but thick, white locks clustered round the base of his head. . . . Gold rimmed spectacles over which he peered, were on top of his nose." Duncan was a businessman by both training and instinct. He saw the benefit of marriage for other people, but ironically did not see how it could help him. He was a confirmed bachelor with no desire to reform until he met Gladys Knowles. When the slender, dainty five-foot-five woman entered the *Matrimonial News* office, Duncan was instantly smitten.

"I could not find my voice for a few moments," he later confessed in an editorial he wrote for his paper. "Her eyes were so honest and intelligent." Gladys broke the silence, greeting him warmly and handing him her advertisement. Duncan assured Gladys that he was "quite capable of finding her the perfect companion." He told her that his publication focused on "aiding people in high life" and that the paper was responsible for forty thousand marriages to date.

The enamored editor offered Gladys a seat and began inquiring about her background. Not long after she shared with him that she lived with her widowed mother in the London borough of Fulham, Duncan asked her to have dinner with him. Over the course of a year, the two courted, and Duncan sent Gladys numerous gifts. Among the more frivolous were a thousand pen-and-ink kisses.

Gladys was moved by his romantic gestures and believed he'd proven his affection was sincere. Any doubts she had about entering into a permanent relationship with him disappeared when he promised to give her $10,000 a year if she would consent to be his wife. In the event of his death, he promised to leave her more than $25,000 a year for the remainder of her life. "What portionless girl could resist such a gold-girt allowance?" the *Daily Tribune* asked readers following the story in early 1891.

Duncan asked Gladys's mother for her hand in marriage, and she consented to the union. He then proposed to Gladys, proudly showing her the marriage license he had acquired. Gladys accepted. The pair decided to get married at Duncan's palatial family home in Sussex in mid-August 1890. Prior to leaving on the trip, he gave Gladys a trousseau worth more than $7,000.

Gladys worked feverishly organizing the wedding. Flowers were selected, guest lists were compiled, dressmakers were consulted about the wedding gown, and a massive cake was ordered. As the big day approached, however, Gladys noticed Duncan was behaving oddly. When she pressed him for a reason, he told her he wanted to postpone the event because the vicar of his parish was not going to be in town for the ceremony. Duncan explained he didn't feel comfortable having the nuptials performed by the curate, the vicar's assistant. Gladys tried to reason with her fiancé, but to no avail. The wedding would be put off a few days.

The modest and proper bride-to-be locked herself in her room each evening. Only after they were husband and wife would Gladys allow Duncan access to her private quarters. Adamant about not waiting, he forced himself into her chambers one evening and tried to take advantage of her. Gladys screamed and demanded to be taken back to her mother's home. Duncan persuaded her to change her mind. After all, "no one wanted the humiliating scene to play out in front of the servants," he reminded her. "We'll be married shortly anyway."

The revised date for the wedding came and went with no vows being exchanged. Duncan claimed he had misplaced the license. A teary-eyed Gladys simply nodded as he promised to take her back to London the following morning so they could be married there. Once they arrived, Duncan changed his mind again and made another excuse for wanting to reschedule the nuptials.

Gladys was embarrassed by the situation and kept to her room in the hotel suite where they were staying. Duncan continued to try to have his way with her. She escaped to one of the bathrooms and announced through the bolted door that if he dared come near her again she would scream the business down.

When Gladys did not return home as her mother expected, Mrs. Elizabeth Knowles marched to the *Matrimonial News* office and demanded to see Duncan. Rumor had spread that Duncan had reconsidered marrying Gladys but that the couple had consummated their relationship. Mrs. Knowles informed Duncan that he would make things right and restore her daughter's honor or suffer the consequences. Time and time again however, Duncan broke the wedding date.

In October 1890, local newspapers revealed that Duncan already had a wife. Two months prior to meeting Gladys, Duncan had said "I do" to Harriet Whyte-Melville. Duncan sent word to Gladys that he was not free to marry her, and he was willing to make restitution for his actions. In truth, Duncan lacked the funds to offer the jilted bride any money at all. He owed a hefty amount in taxes and was on the verge of filing bankruptcy. Gladys informed Duncan that she would only be satisfied if he would divorce Harriet and marry her. She told him she would find work and support them both if he would take her as his wife. Duncan was either unwilling or unable to accommodate Gladys.

Heartbroken and her reputation maligned, Gladys decided to sue for breach of promise. During the highly publicized trial, Gladys's attorney characterized Duncan as "an artful seducer of great experience." The lawyer claimed Duncan had knowingly corrupted an innocent girl. He disclosed to the jury the insincere groom had been married a total of four times and fathered seven illegitimate children with six different women. He also let the court know Duncan's age was in fact seventy-seven and not sixty-three as he had told Gladys.

The court found in favor of Gladys and awarded her $10,000 in damages. Duncan's lawyers then filed an appeal claiming the amount was excessive. The court agreed to reduce the cost to $7,500. Duncan transferred the interest in the *Matrimonial News* and left the country.

The reporter covering the story of the misleading marital agent for the *Pall Mall Gazette* concluded the article on the matter by noting, "If marriages are made in heaven, St. Peter has a very odd deputy in the proprietor of the *Matrimonial News*."

In October 1891, Duncan was arrested for nonpayment of debts. Several notices were sent to the former marital agent informing him of a hearing scheduled to collect what he owed, but he refused to appear. The prosecution asked why Duncan had failed to appear. His attorney spoke for him, apologizing for his actions. He explained that his client was an old man suffering from sciatica and requested the court's indulgence. The prosecuting attorney reluctantly agreed but demanded Duncan answer for himself. He was sworn in, and the questions began.

"You have been the editor of the *Matrimonial News* for many years?" the lawyer asked Duncan.

"I have," he replied.

"Were you also the proprietor for the *Matrimonial News?*" the attorney further queried.

"Yes, I was also the proprietor of the paper," he responded.

"What has been the average income?" the prosecuting attorney pressed.

"It varied from time to time. Two years it was $700," Duncan answered. "About ten years ago I made $4,200. Last year I made no profit at all."

"Did you keep an account of the income?" the prosecuting attorney probed.

"No, I did not," Duncan told the court. "I had only myself to consider, and the books were never balanced."

The witness said he could not remember when he received the bankruptcy notice, but it was sent through his solicitor. Duncan offered up several reasons for not paying his creditors or Gladys Knowles for the breach of promise suit. He told the court he had no liquid assets and needed time to sell some property in order to make good on the amount owed. He also stated that he was waiting on money owed to him to be paid.

Duncan denied having any money, houses, or land in other countries. The point was argued, and his attorney finally relayed that any funds that once belonged to his client were now in Duncan's son's name and, as such, could not be used to pay his bills. He had transferred ownership of the *Matrimonial News* publication to his son as well. Duncan did admit to selling several pieces of furniture and other personal items for $850. When the prosecutor queried him about those funds, he told them that he gave the money away to two women he felt could benefit from a monetary gift. He could not remember where they lived and had not seen them since he gave them the funds.

At the conclusion of the hearing, the court was not satisfied that Duncan had made a reasonable attempt to pay his debt. He was found in contempt of court and taken into custody. He was later sentenced to four years of penal servitude. Duncan passed away on November 21, 1913, at the age of ninety-two.

Hannah Gould

The Stampeder

The crew and passengers aboard the steamship the *City of Colum-bia* stood huddled together on the flooded deck of the vessel. Night was all around them, and an awful moment of peril and suspense hung in the wet air. A perfect storm had overtaken the steamer, and raging winds had driven her into a mass of rocks. She was stranded in the Strait of Magellan, and plans were underway to off-load a group of women fortune hunters on their way to Alaska to the rocks that flanked the ship on either side.

Mrs. Hannah S. Gould, the matriarch of the group of women travelers, anxiously waited for instructions about what needed to be done from the *City of Columbia*'s captain, E. C. Baker. Wearing anxious expressions, forty-five ladies surrounded Hannah. They pressed in closely to her, waiting. They were ready to put into action the command passed from the captain to them from Hannah.

All of the women with Hannah had responded to an invitation she issued in the *New York Times* in early 1897. The fifty-year-old Long Island native had organized the unusual expedition, of which the primary focus was to financially support miners stampeding north to the Klondike River. More than five hundred ladies applied to take part in the expedition, but fewer than fifty were selected to go. Several of the women hoped to find husbands among the prospectors in Alaska, as well as their own gold strikes.

Hannah, who had assumed responsibility for her husband's many business ventures when he passed away in 1891, was an ambitious woman eager to prove herself capable of adding to the fortune she had acquired. "I received all my business training from my father," she told a reporter with the *Frank Leslie's Illustrated Weekly* magazine in December 1897. "He trained me the same as though I had been a boy, not only in finance and mathematics, but in firearms."

Hannah's experience in the business field included ventures in real estate investing and the building of rail lines. According to the December 30, 1897, edition of *Frank Leslie's Illustrated Weekly*, she supervised the building of the Middleton, Georgia and Atlantic Railway. The construction of the 138-mile line included bridges and trestlework. Fascinated by her efforts, the *Frank Leslie's Illustrated Weekly* magazine reporter inquired how she managed to accomplish such feats as a woman. "If a woman is practical and has the physical strength of a man she can build a railroad as well as a man can," Hannah informed him. "I believe I must be the only woman to date who became a railroad contractor, and I ran an iron car and worked with the men. If it were necessary for me to take hold with the men I did it."

Dealing with men on a professional level was all Hannah had in mind when she conceived the idea of joining the Alaskan Gold Rush. Nevertheless, "some women who will be accompanying me on this expedition want to marry," Hannah confessed to *Frank Leslie's Illustrated Weekly*, "but they have been told this trip isn't like that." Regardless of the purely economic reasons for which the mission was designed, several bachelorettes on the journey were determined to find a mate. Indeed, some members of her group had responded to ads from eligible men seeking wives. One of the ads posted in a San Francisco newspaper that had caught the attention of a few of the ladies traveling with Hannah read, "Wanted – lady of good social standing temporarily in reduced circumstances wants to meet honorable gentlemen bound for Klondike ward. Object business and ultimate matrimonial partnership."

Among the ladies of good social standing selected to be a part of the expedition was Hannah's own unmarried daughter, Kate, and Miss Margaret Henderson from Pittsburgh, Pennsylvania. Using the riches she inherited from her father, Margaret planned to open a hotel and supply miners with mining tools. Four other affluent women with the party were trained nurses who would take charge of the hospital Hannah planned to build. According to the December 30, 1897, edition of *Frank Leslie's Illustrated Weekly,* Hannah was a "capital physician, as well as an expert nurse." Hannah shared with the *Weekly,* "Our hospital department will include everything from stretchers and medicines down to bandages and surgical implements. And if there is no use for a hospital we will convert it into a boarding house."

Hannah would not consider any woman over the age of fifty-one or under the age of twenty-one to join the expedition. "Neither will I take a woman who has marriage in primary view. To such I say there is degradation enough there already." She made that statement in part as a response to merchants in Dawson City who thought the expedition was a bad idea. Those who earned a living auctioning off willing women as wives felt Hannah's group would threaten their business. Emphasizing the true intent of the voyage calmed their worries.

The women Hannah selected to travel with her to Alaska had to meet a physical requirement as well as an age parameter. "They must possess strength and courage and be able to withstand the hardships in store for them," she shared with the *New York Times* in August 1897.

The forty-five women in Hannah's party were each charged $800 to make the trip. The expedition's leader promised to back the travelers financially once in the Klondike, if needed, until they could each stake a paying claim, at which point half of the proceeds would revert to Hannah as custodian of the capital. All were supplied with clothing designed for winter in the Arctic region. Each outfit consisted of bloomers lined with lamb's wool, a fur coat, fur leggings, and fur hood, a rubber coat and boots, hats, gingham gown, sunbonnet, shirtwaists, and linen shirts. Whatever fineries party members felt they needed to attract a husband were left up to them. With the exception of one long dress to be used for state occasions, Hannah tried to discourage such frivolities as well as the notion of finding a husband through advertisements. "I cannot possibly forbid such mail-order unions," she told *Frank Leslie's Illustrated Weekly*, "but I cannot recommend it. Do I expect them to marry? There may be some marriages, but in no case have I looked with favor upon a woman whom I suspected might be seeking adventure in that direction. They are, without exception, all earnest, right-minded women on this expedition, whose aim and purpose is simply that of gaining a fortune in exactly the same way as the men do."

The steamship *City of Columbia* set sail from New York with Hannah and her female party on December 17, 1897. One hundred thirty-six days later the vessel arrived in Seattle. Stops had been made en route at Saint Thomas, Barbados, and Rio. At the various anchoring places the passengers amused themselves with the wild natives that gathered around the ship. On February 8, 1898, the storm that overtook the *City of Columbia* forced her onto the rocks not far from Valparaiso, Chile. The ship was hopelessly stuck with several hooks in her hull from other vehicles that had tried to rescue her. The cost to repair the ship and get her on her way again was estimated to be $25,000. Hannah eventually paid for the repairs to be made, and, after twenty-two days of being grounded, the crew, staff, and passengers were off on their way again to Washington State.

Hannah and her party arrived in Seattle in early May 1898. From there, two of Hannah's cousins who were living in the area provided the women with the steam launch to transport the group to the Yukon. During the stopover in the Washington Territory some members of the expedition had managed to acquire copies of newspapers containing a variety of ads posted by Alaskan gold miners seeking wives. When word reached Hannah that the subject of marriage was a popular topic among the ladies, she reiterated of the true purpose of the trip. "We are going to help succor the starving miners in the Klondike and add to their stock of worldly possessions," she told the women. "We are grub-stakers foremost. If a miner has no money to live on we will provide the necessities, receiving in return a certain percentage of his ore."

Unbeknownst to the women in the expedition, Hannah had already declined a marriage proposal from a persistent Chilean hired by her to repair the *City of Columbia*. No matter how tempted she might have been, she refused to allow herself to be distracted from the goal in which she had become so heavily invested.

The expedition arrived in Alaska in late May 1898. Dawson City's population grew that day from 3,011 to 3,057: three thousand men and fifty-seven women. Although many of the ladies in Hannah's party successfully provided miners with the funds to locate and stake a claim, a number of these same women married quickly, including Margaret Henderson. Hannah concentrated on the hospital and mission she established. Her position on marriage gradually softened: She confessed to a reporter in 1899 that she would "consider a gold millionaire's proposal to wed, if made, and his disciplines echoed the same view as her own."

Want-Ad Brides

In 1744, Benjamin Franklin published the first mail-order catalog selling scientific and academic books. The success of the product prompted other business owners to create their own publications, selling everything from underwear to surgical instruments. By the turn of the century there were hundreds of mail-order books available to consumers, including the Montgomery Ward and Sears Roebuck and Co. catalogs.

The majority of catalogs included a guarantee to customers, which invited those who weren't completely satisfied to return any item for a full refund. Matrimonial publications not only were unable to make such an offer but also unwilling to give any money back to unhappy shoppers.

The increased popularity of mail-order bride periodicals made it difficult for some to be noticed. In 1905, the average such publication was 320 pages long and contained more than two hundred photographs. Simple advertisements no longer grabbed a bachelor or bachelorette's immediate attention.

Men and women desperate to find a spouse began to seek out different venues. Some posted flyers at railway depots, and others placed want ads in local newspapers. These want ads were often found in the same section with promotions for various cure-alls and wonder drugs. Smaller newspapers sold advertising space for a fraction of what it would cost to place the same ad in a publication specifically geared toward matrimony. In addition to saving money, hopeful singles believed their advertisements stood a better chance at getting noticed. With less competition vying for the reader's attention, want-ad brides were more confident of a marriage proposal.

Whether they used mail-order catalogs or want ads, prospective brides could not predict the results of their postings. An outcome could be bittersweet, the start of a relationship that would last a lifetime, or a comical circumstance that would lead to divorce.

The front page of the April 22, 1913, edition of the *Oakland Tribune* contained a want-ad bride story that was funny to everyone except the newlyweds. After ten days of married life, Alice Richardson Kline decided to leave her husband Simon Kline because he was a smoker.

Kline had specifically noted when he answered Alice's want ad that he "abstained from all tobacco products." She found out that was a lie less than two hours after the wedding ceremony had been performed. Simon had been untruthful about his past as well. Alice was not only upset about being lied to, but she was furious that he didn't give her a wedding ring and that he was wearing a suit of rented clothing. "He picked me for a good thing and a meal ticket, but he got fooled. I tried him out and he fell short," Alice told the *Oakland Tribune* reporter.

Mr. Kline and the widowed Mrs. Richardson began corresponding in February 1913 and were married on April 17 of the same year. Simon was initially drawn to Alice's want ad because she was a widow with means who could cook. "He knew a good thing when he met me," she informed the newspaper.

He proposed the first night we met. The broken promise I made to accept him for better or worse has been offset by his own prevarications. In the first place he married me in another man's clothes which he borrowed. He neglected to get me a ring and I had to use the one my second husband gave me. When I sought a husband I specifically stated that he must not be a user of tobacco in any form; within a few days I found him using snuff and chewing tobacco. I also discovered that his [sic] is a deserter from the United States Navy where he served under the name of Oscar King about ten years ago. He told me that the government did not want him anymore, as ten years had expired.

Well I got tired the other day, so I thought that I would test him. He came home Sunday night about dinner time. I had baked a batch of bread and there was plenty to eat in the house but I didn't put it on the table. He asked me if there wasn't anything to eat. "Where is my supper," he says to me. "Well," I said, "when you bring home the bacon I'll cook it, and not until then." With that he showed himself to his true light. I said that I would be willing to cook anything from a steak to a lion, or anything else like that if he would bring it home. He wanted to know why I didn't ask him for money. I told him I was too proud to ask him for money and besides, I said, you are a smoker!

The Klines' problems escalated from there. Alice eventually sought the counsel of the deputy district attorney for a way to get rid of her husband legally.

An overdue shave lost Pat O'Brien of Waukee, Iowa, his young and pretty want-ad bride. Pat's whiskers—or the lack of them—caused widow Margaret Lafferty to halt at the church door and refuse to take the vow to love and obey a man who looked like he had been dunked in a kettle of boiling water.

Pat was lonely on his farm near Waukee. He knew little of gambling on the matrimonial market and asked a friend from Des Moines for advice on the subject. This friend saw his opportunity to play a joke and promptly put an advertisement in one of the local papers. The advertisement was misleading because it pictured the farmer as young and smooth shaven.

For forty-plus years Pat had been growing a beard, and his whiskers had been allowed to grow at will. Knowing this, his friend made the pictures that more alluring and comical by representing him to any prospective bride as a beardless youth. Margaret saw the advertisement and was so attracted by the description of the young Iowa farmer that she immediately applied as a candidate. Letters were exchanged, and finally the pair made arrangements to meet in Des Moines and get married.

To live up to the requirements of the advertisement, Pat got a shave. The beard came off along with patches of cuticle. As a farmer Pat was sunburned everywhere but under the beard, which had protected the lower portion of his face from the sun and the wind for years. As a result, the freshly-shorn skin was as smooth and soft as a baby's. The contrast was startling, but ignorant of that fact, Pat met his intended bride at the train station after his shave and introduced himself. The bride was horrified at his facial patch-work and mentioned the fact to Pat's friend, who was to be the best man at the wedding ceremony.

Pat and the best man learned the bride had run away when she didn't show up at the church to get the necessary license.

Seventy-three-year-old bridegroom William H. Burden couldn't have been happier with his want-ad bride. In October 1915, Burden bragged to the *Altoona Miner* in Altoona, Pennsylvania, that "no cupid can beat the newspaper cupid." Burden had a three-day experience with a want-ad bride and was thrilled with the way things turned out.

Twenty-six-year-old Lulu Douglas Thompson from Atlanta, Georgia, had responded to an advertisement placed in the paper by Burden, and, after one letter between them, Burden traveled from Pennsylvania to meet and possibly marry her. Once Burden locked eyes with Thompson, he knew they were meant to be together. He immediately proposed, and Miss Thompson accepted.

The sharp contrast in age attracted the attention of a reporter at the *Altoona Mirror* who, hearing about the duo, sought them out for an interview. Thompson, the beauty that won Burden's heart as well as his vast fortune, approved all her elderly husband had to say about entrusting your heart to the care of the advertising columns. "When a man wants something it is natural for him to advertise for it," Burden bragged. "Why should my marriage cause such a fuss? I simply was a widower who had enjoyed a happy married life and wanted to try it again. Yes, it was a romance, but all I can say about that part of it is that I knew Miss Thompson well enough and long enough to marry her. My friends were surprised, but I'm old enough to take care of myself. No one opposed our marriage because no one knew about it until it happened."

Burden's son, a middle-aged man, was happy his father had found someone to love and to love him in return.

"What do I think of want-ad marriages?" Mrs. Burden was asked by the newspaper reporter. "Nothing except that I'm very, very happy," she told them.

Rev. John R. Bailey and Margaret Coon shared the same sentiment. Bailey hailed from Colorado, and Coon was from Decatur, Illinois. The couple was married at the home of the bride on August 24, 1897. According to the August 25, 1897, edition of the *Decatur Review*, "the bride is 60 years old and the groom has passed his 65th year, both have married children and are well cared for."

The wedding was brought about through the instrumentality of a want ad placed in the *Daily Alta California* newspaper. The bride and groom did not meet until four days before they were married, but they had corresponded for a long time and learned a great deal about one another through their letters. Bailey came to Decatur to meet the woman he had fallen in love with via mail. "There was no disappointment on either side," he boasted.

Immigrants from Asia living at opposite ends of the United States depended on want ads at times to help end their solitary lives. Miss Fong Jean Leen, a graduate of the Woman's Occidental College in Philadelphia, and Wone Fore, a Baptist missionary working in San Francisco's Chinatown, were married on January 1, 1915.

A want ad that Leen placed in the *Daily Alta California* newspaper brought the pair together, and they corresponded for quite some time. Leen did not see the bridegroom until a few days before their wedding. Wone had sent a photograph of himself to her, and she knew him the moment she saw him. She was very complimentary of his looks and told him the picture did not do him justice. Wone returned the flowery praise.

The bride wore a flowing gown brought from Hong Kong. The couple was married at the First Chinese Baptist Church in San Francisco. The ceremony was performed in both Chinese and English. Decorations were Asian. The guests included Christianized Chinese and Americans interested in mission work.

After a short honeymoon in Monterey, California, the pair returned to San Francisco where they told the newspaper they "planned to live happily in love always and grateful for want-ads."

Most everyone who longed for a companion and dared to make their decision known in an advertisement hoped for the same good fortune.

Runaway Brides

After spending long periods of time reviewing numerous advertisements listed in various matrimonial publications, men and women responded to the announcements they felt best suited their needs, crossed their fingers, and prayed for a favorable outcome. In the early 1900s there was a series of mail-order brides who accepted proposals from men and soon after regretted their decision.

Failed attempts to find a spouse via postings in magazines and newspapers were widely publicized, which thrilled critics of the popular method of finding a spouse. Religious leaders and suffragettes believed matrimonial periodicals degraded the sanctity of marriage and promoted the idea that women were nothing more than commodities to be traded. They hoped reports of unhappy first meetings and fraud would put an end to the mail-order bride and groom business.

Men and women had a tendency to misrepresent themselves in paid announcements. According to the periodical *Hand and Heart*—a family, social, and temperance magazine—more dissatisfied couples appeared in court to settle breach of promise claims between 1905 and 1921 than pursued any other civil suit during the same period.

On August 11, 1908, the *Hutchinson Daily News* in Hutchinson, Kansas, ran an article about a jilted groom who had filed charges against the mail-order bride business and the federal government, claiming that the US Postal Service was being used to defraud prospective spouses. Clyde Williamson, a resident of Seattle, Washington, read an advertisement in a western matrimonial paper in April 1906 and decided to write to the woman who was seeking a husband in the ad. Williamson noted in his complaint that the young woman in the case gave him inaccurate information about her appearance, disposition, and family. "The courtship of the couple consisted of an even 100 letters," the newspaper report read.

Williamson insisted that, in his correspondence with the intended, he inquired about her home life and character. "She led me to believe and that it would be her object in life to make her husband a 'loving and useful helpmate,'" Williamson reported. He also noted that, once he met her in person, he felt he was "grossly deceived" and that the woman in question was nothing like she presented herself to be in the ad.

Although Bessie Stouthard did not think the Postal Service was at fault in her situation, the mail-order bride from Kentucky felt that she, too, was misled by an advertisement. Henry Clay King had placed an ad in the *New Plan Company* catalog that caught her attention, but it turned out he was less than honest about his age. Stouthard had no idea King was more than thirty years older than she was until they were married within an hour of meeting.

King had advertised for a wife in the summer of 1911 and received six hundred answers from every corner of the country. Shortly after they wed, Stouthard left to visit her family and never returned. King filed for divorce on the basis of desertion.

Many would-be spouses were disappointed in the mail-order bride system, but their circumstances never warranted litigation. One such person was Edith Kish, who posted an announcement in the *Matrimonial News* in February 1913. John Kissel, the owner of a hotel in Linton, Oregon, promptly responded to the prospective bride's advertisement. The two communicated via letter for months before Kissel sent Kish a diamond ring and asked her to marry him. She happily accepted and traveled west to meet her future husband. After one glance at Kissel, Kish told him he was not her ideal and returned the ring.

Charles K. Afflack of Muskogee, Oklahoma, was the subject of much gossip in his hometown when he selected a want-ad bride in early 1913 from the *Halcyon Matrimonial Company*. Shortly after the pair exchanged vows, Afflack told friends and family he noticed a remarkable change in the woman he had corresponded with from Maine. The couple divorced, and Afflack eventually married a woman he met through a friend.

Thirteen days after George C. Ganabrant of Monroe, Michigan, married a mail-order bride from Arkansas, the woman ran away from him. "We had become acquainted by mail," he told a reporter at the *Orange County Times Press* newspaper on March 22, 1915. "We were married on December 5, 1913, after I paid $50 to bring her from her home in Hot Springs." Two weeks later George's wife informed him she had to go to Colorado on business. She asked her husband for a loan of $500 to take care of the taxes on a piece of property in Denver. He refused to give her the sum, but did furnish the $75 she needed to make the trip.

George kept his money stored about the house he briefly shared with his bride. Once she had left for Colorado, he went searching for his funds and learned his duplicitous wife had stolen all the cash he had. "She also went shopping on her way out of town at the local merchants and charged more than $60 to my account," he complained to the newspaper. One of the items she purchased with George's money was a gold ring.

On March 11, 1912, the *Stevens Point Daily Journal* in Stevens Point, Wisconsin, posted a story about the risks involved with meeting a potential husband or wife through a want ad. The article, entitled "Californian Lost a Mail Order Bride," described what happened to a farmer after he arrived to collect his future wife from the train station in Holtville, California.

After he had paid all the expenses of her divorce from her first husband, purchased tickets for her and her mother to Holts-ville, California, where they were to be married, and agreed to allow her mother to live with them, Mrs. Minnie May DeWitt quarreled with J. A. Ray and refused to marry him.

Instead, Mrs. DeWitt is said to be preparing now to marry a young man whom she met before she began correspondence with Ray, whose acquaintance she had made through a mat-rimonial paper. Ray has returned to his California home. He said he had no feeling against Mrs. DeWitt, even if she had changed her mind and called him a "jay."

Mrs. DeWitt is a pretty little woman eighteen years old. She was married three years ago, and about two years ago, after the birth of a daughter, she brought suit for divorce. Not hav-ing the money to pay the court costs, she allowed the case to rest on the docket. Meantime she had become acquainted, it is said, with a young man here and they desired to marry, but neither had the money for the cost of the divorce. One day Mrs. DeWitt saw Ray's name in a matrimonial paper. She began a correspondence with him and learned that he was forty-three years old and the owner of a fine irrigate farm near El Sentro. He wrote interesting letters and so did she. Photographs were exchanged and finally they arranged to marry. Ray sent a gen-erous check to Mrs. DeWitt toward the expense of her wedding outfit and a few days later arrived to claim his bride.

There was still the divorce to be obtained however. Ray paid all the expenses of Mrs. DeWitt's side of the case and sat in court during the hearing. It had been planned to have the wedding here, but when Judge Sapp prohibited Mrs. DeWitt from marrying again for six months that caused a change in the plans.

A reception was given instead of a wedding, so the guests were not entirely disappointed. Preparations were made at

once to start to California where the ceremony would be per-
formed. "But I couldn't think of going way out there and leav-
ing mother at home alone," said Mrs. DeWitt. "We'll take
mother right along with us," said Mr. Ray.

A number of friends gathered at the house to wish the
party a pleasant journey. And then Mrs. DeWitt and Mr. Ray
quarreled.

Mrs. DeWitt said Mr. Ray was a "jay," that she would not
walk down the street with him, let alone be married to him.
Mr. Ray took the first train for California after having turned
in the two tickets to Holtville which he had purchased for his
prospective wife and mother-in-law.

J. A. Ray wouldn't be the last man to be taken advantage of by
a disreputable mail-order bride. In 1921, a groom in Washington
State sent a train ticket and money to Missouri for his fiancée to
join him at his homestead, but she never arrived.

Frank Everett, a rancher from Chester, Washington, answered
an ad he found in Matrimonial News *and after a brief time*
corresponding, proposed to the lady. At her request, Everett dis-
patched a fat envelope to her containing, among other things,
the price of a first class ticket including sleeping car accommoda-
tions and $25 for expenses from Kansas City to Spokane where
Everett was to meet her.

The bride was due to arrive in Spokane on March 15,
but she never made it. Everett waited five days for his fiancé
[sic] before he had to admit to himself he'd been jilted. "The
girl, whose name I shall not make public described herself as
twenty-four years of age, fairly good looking and a first class
cook," Everett told a reporter with the Bismarck Daily Tribune. *"She wanted to come west and marry a rancher, but I*
guess she changed her mind after getting my money. I've been

*'bunked' and I'm going back to the ranch, but before I promise
again to marry I'm going to see the other party on the ground."*

Robert Miller of Denver experienced the same kind of disappointment at the hand of his "correspondence bride" Eliza Kent
in August 1906. In spite of Miller's best efforts to keep the arrival
of his betrothed a secret between his closest associates, more than
a few curious people were on hand at the train station to meet
Kent.

She was wearing an elegant traveling suit and had a rose pinned
to her lapel so Miller could easily identify her. Miller barely had
a chance to introduce himself when the crowd that had gathered
began pressing in around Eliza. The two exchanged a glance and he
smiled at her, but she did not return the favor. She was not pleased
with Miller's appearance, and she backed away from the scene. The
crowd followed her. They pursued her for six blocks until she managed to hide out inside a stranger's home. The following day she
boarded a train back from where she came.

Some mail-order bride experiences appeared at first as though
they were destined to fail, but fate intervened. Marie E. Grey and
J. E. Guy were scheduled to be married on March 7, 1921, in
Spokane, Washington. Their romance had its origins in the advertisement column of an eastern paper. Guy waited for his intended
to step off the train, but Marie was nowhere to be seen. As the
vehicle was pulling out of the station the mail-order bride jumped
out of one of the cars. She had gotten the tie on her shoe tangled
in a section of the underside of her seat and had trouble getting
it undone.

Guy and Grey hurried off to the First Presbyterian Church
and were married. Guy, who was an expert machinist in the
employ of the Potlatch Lumber Company in northern Idaho, said
when he read Grey's advertisement he knew she was right for him.
"She was a widow, and lonely, and tired of owning herself, and

wanted a man and responsible mate," he told the *Bismarck* (ND) *Daily Tribune.* After six months of corresponding, Grey agreed to marry Guy. The couple made their home in the town of Potlatch and served as a positive example to their friends and neighbors who considered the success rate of mail-order marriages to be extremely low.

Fred Harvey

Gentlemen Matrimony Agent

More than two dozen women adorned in black poplin skirts with matching blouses, stiff white collars, and aprons and sporting sleek, shiny hair fashioned into a tidy bun, busily hurried about a Santa Fe Railroad restaurant in Albuquerque, New Mexico, in 1879. The gruff, rugged cowhands who were the patrons of the establishment looked out of place at tables covered with European linens, cut crystal glasses, and fine china place settings. Dressed in their Sunday suits, the men were on their best behavior as they waited patiently for the exceptional food they were about to be served. The reason for dusting off their manners and sitting up straight with their unruly hair slicked back had more to do with the waitresses serving them than with the food or ambience.

The attentive waitstaff were known as the Harvey Girls. They were part of an elite group of women brought to the coarse West to offer culture and fine dining to a part of America devoid of such experiences. Another important component to the venture, started by English businessman Fred Harvey in 1876, was the possibility of matrimony. Harvey's first chain of restaurants was geared toward railroad passengers and cowboys lacking sophistication. It was Harvey's hope to civilize the Wild West not only with good food but also by introducing polite, well-groomed single women to bachelors living on the lonely frontier.

One of the most interesting and important results of Harvey's system was the matrimonial feature. He insisted upon having good-looking waitresses, and most of them were selected by his sister in Michigan with that attribute in mind. According to the May 18, 1891, edition of the *Albuquerque Morning Journal* newspaper, of the five- to six-thousand individuals Harvey employed, more than half were women. They came from various eastern cities and were looking for jobs as well as husbands. Fred Harvey acted as a matrimonial agent of sorts.

The Harvey Girls were noted for neatness of dress, modest demeanor, and graceful manners. They looked very attractive to ranchers, miners, and other bachelors who often didn't see a woman more than twice a year. The girls were housed in dormitories presided over by housemothers. They were looked over as carefully as boarding-school students at the female seminaries in the East. Many of the Harvey Girls were former schoolteachers. They worked twelve-hour shifts and made twelve to twenty-five dollars a month. They were provided room and board, as well as vacation and travel expenses. Will Rogers is quoted as saying in 1968 that "Fred Harvey and his girls kept the West in food and wives." One legend perpetuated by Rogers was that twenty thousand of the comely waitresses wound up as brides to western ranchers, cowboys, and railroad men.

Harvey never expected to keep a girl more than three or four months and encouraged the marriage of his employees provided the grooms were sober and honorable men. He took great satisfaction in the happiness and prosperity of his protégés, and the population in every town along the line of the Santa Fe Railroad from Missouri to California included boys named after him. Some of the waitresses did indeed marry very well. One became the wife of the richest ranchman in northern Texas; others married cattlemen

A group of Harvey Girls standing in the dining room of the Harvey House in Ash Fork, Arizona, in 1916.   KANSAS STATE HISTORICAL SOCIETY

of large means and had bright futures. Those girls who did marry well encouraged other girls from their hometowns to come and take a chance. Every one of them became a perpetual employment agent for Fred Harvey, who never refused a place to an industrious, good-looking girl.

With the exception of one tense situation that occurred in Deming, New Mexico, in 1910, neither Harvey nor his girls experienced trouble in any of his establishments. A report in the May 18, 1911, edition of the *Albuquerque Morning Journal* described a witness's recall of the scene that played out between Fred Harvey and a few boisterous cowboys.

One day shortly after we had opened up the hotel and res-
taurant a party of cowboys traveling from Las Vegas, New

Mexico invaded the business and they were full of beer. They started riding around the park in which the restaurant was situated, yelling and shooting off their guns. Mr. Harvey, who was taking his dinner, stood it for a while but finally threw down his napkin and started for the scene of the trouble. Before he got into the park the cowboys were off their horses and had gone into the billiard room where Pete, a six-foot westerner, who also had a saloon in Kansas City, was bartending.

Pete was a native fellow and had decorated his bar with Indian relics and various curios he had picked up in his travels. The cowboys got onto them at once and began shooting up the curios. Then they began shooting at the bottles on the sidebar to see if they could shoot the necks off, and were engaged in that activity when Mr. Harvey entered. He grasped the situation and turned to face the men boldly he said to them in a friendly tone, "Boy, put up your guns." One of the cowboys snapped back, "Who the hell are you?" "My name is Fred Harvey," Harvey replied, "and I own this place and will not have any rowdiness here. You are welcome to come here as often as you please and stay as long as you like as long as you behave like gentlemen. But if you don't act like gentlemen you can't stay and you can't come again. Now, damn you, put up your guns and have a drink with Fred Harvey."

One of the men called Red John, who worked at the hotel afterwards, commenced to cursing and Harvey grabbed him by his collar, jerked him over the counter and held him down on the floor sternly and said, "You mustn't swear in this place." Just then one of the cowboys called out, "Fred Harvey is a gentleman" and that ended the dispute. Mr. Harvey set up drinks for them and invited them to breakfast. They accepted Harvey's generous offer but insisted they cook for him. They burst into the kitchen, lined all the waitresses against a wall and made them *watch as they prepared the meal. Red John happened to meet the Harvey Girl he would go on to marry that day.*

Fred Harvey was born in 1835 and started his restaurant business with the Santa Fe Railroad in 1876. By 1900, Harvey's company was running fifteen hotels, forty-seven restaurants, and thirty dining cars. The Harvey family continued to run the company until 1968, when it was sold to the AmFac Corporation. According to the February 14, 1988, edition of the *Santa Fe New Mexican*, "Harvey's combination of fine cuisine, superb service and feminine charm helped settle and civilize the American West. What had been seen as a hostile and inhospitable land was transformed into an exotic leisure destination thanks to him and his girls."

Fred Harvey died in 1901 at the age of sixty-six.

Happily Ever After

Business for matrimonial publications increased substantially whenever stories of successful mail-order connections were reported. Editors for periodicals such as *Matrimonial News* and the *New Plan Company* catalog shared happily-ever-after tales with daily newspapers in hopes they would print the romantic adventures of correspondence couples.

Several such stories appeared in newspapers like the *Waterloo Daily Courier* in Waterloo, Iowa, and the *North Adams Evening Transcript* in North Adams, Massachusetts, around Valentine's Day in 1905. Advertisements printed alongside the mail-order articles were placed by florists, jewelers, and chocolate makers. According to a post in the February 6, 1905, edition of the *Waterloo Evening Courier,* readership for the paper doubled on romantic holidays like Saint Valentine's Day and Christmas. "Whenever mail-order love stories are printed, and particularly those that present a high view of matrimony and the fun couples could have in a happy marriage," the editorial staff at the *Courier* noted, "the circulation grows."

An article entitled "Would She Bother Him?" which ran on Sunday, February 10, 1905, was an example of a story that generated significant business for the Iowa paper.

Martin Perkins, aged forty-one, and Eliza Gulless, aged thirty-seven, sat before an open wood fire, he holding his hands, she knitting. For two years the couple corresponded via mail then came the day Mr. Perkins asked Miss Gulless to come west. Miss Gulless, now Mrs. Perkins, agreed. Mr. Perkins resided in the area of Bisbee, Arizona. The future Mrs. Perkins left her parents and siblings behind in Ohio to join him. The two met through a mail-order advertisement.

Twice a week for ten months the pair met. On Wednesday they were together at the church for choir practice and Saturday evenings were spent at Miss Gulless's home talking and getting to know each other further. Mr. Perkins lived with his mother and half the people in the Bisbee area said it would be a shame for him to marry and leave his mother alone, the other half maintained he was morally bound to marry Miss Gulless.

During the ten months they spent together Mr. Perkins was endeavoring to make up his mind that it would be safe for a man of his confirmed habits to enter matrimony. He sat with Miss Gulless engaged in the same occupation every week—holding his hands with the occasional twirling of his thumbs—while Miss Gulless knitted. But at last he had come to the determination to ask her to become his wife.

"Miss Liza," he began, "marriage is a fearful thing when it doesn't turn out well."

"I think very likely it must be."

"They say marriages late in life seldom turn out well."

"Do they?"

"Yes, they say when a man has passed forty he's set in his ways and a woman always around, interfering with him, is very hard to bear."

He took out his handkerchief and wiped his temples as though the little picture he had drawn indicated hot weather. Miss Gulless seemed more than usually absorbed in her knitting and made no reply for some time. Then she said softly: "If a man gets a sensible woman she wouldn't interfere with him much."

"I've thought often of that. I didn't believe you, for instance, would make it hard for a man."

"It's very nice of you to say so," replied Miss Gulless bending over her work.

"Then you're mighty steady. Some women are flighty. You can never pin them down to anything. If you was to tell me you would do a thing I wouldn't have to argue it with you all over again. I could rely on your doing it same as if it was done."

"I hope I would," replied Miss Gulless meekly.

"Now, I tell you, Miss Liza, there ain't no other woman that lived that I'd take a risk on. I've known you for close to three years and the man who gets you will get a jewel. I would like to be that man. I often think how wonderful it would be to have you flittin' about like a yellow bird among the branches. Will you do it, Miss Liza?"

"Do what?" she asked in a scarcely audible tone.

"Marry me."

She bent lower and lower without reply. He went to her, folded her in his arms, and she whispered "Yes." She kissed him gently on his cheek and added, "I would never be a bother to you."

"I have every confidence of that, Miss Liza," Mr. Perkins nodded.

In June 1904, Mr. Perkins's mother died from complications with her heart. Miss Gulless and Mr. Perkins were wed on November 18, 1904.

The *North Adams Evening Transcript* had similar good fortune with sales of the February 10, 1906, edition of their paper. The article entitled "Matchmaking" was so well received the newspaper sold out, and editors of the *Transcript* were forced to issue a second printing.

According to the *Transcript* article, Joshua Wilson had spent the evening with several friends in the gold-mining area of Coloma, California. It seemed to him he had talked nonstop about the mail-order bride he had been writing to who lived in Maine. In the spring of 1891, Wilson had placed an ad in the matrimonial page of a newspaper, and Cydra Davidson, the daughter of a physician, had written expressing an interest in him. She asked if they might exchange letters and photographs. For more than a year Wilson and Davidson wrote one another. On May 10, 1892, the mail-order groom asked for Davidson's hand in marriage and promised to be a husband she could depend on. Davidson accepted and within a short time of the proposal made the pilgrimage to meet the man who would be her spouse.

Cydra Davidson and Joshua Wilson were to meet for the first time in person at a wedding reception being held at a home next to the Emmanuel Church in Coloma. At the conclusion of the service, Wilson filtered out of the church with the others in attendance and made his way to the reception.

"The drawing room was crowded," the article quoted Wilson.

I looked about for Miss Davidson and spied her in the far corner. By slow small stages I made my way toward her. She marked my approach with a wistful face, and when I was close made room for me. Poor nervous thing! We shook hands and I noted a tender light in her eyes.

"How hot is it here," she asked after we introduced ourselves formally.

"These gatherings can be very warm. Shall we take our conversation outside?" I suggested. We slowly made our way around the people standing in the room until we finally made it to the door and exited.

"How pleasant it is out here," Miss Davidson offered.

"So cool," I responded.

Conversation was slow to get started. We were both careful and Miss Davidson sheepish.

"You are a fine looking woman," I told her respectfully.

"How glad I am to hear it," Miss Davidson replied. "I'm happy to be here. The object of our first love is so rarely the person to make us really happy," she told me.

"First love is the only love," said I.

A great silence fell upon us. I knew it was my moment to tell her how much I loved her. I reached for her hand once I spoke the words and she returned the sentiment then we smiled at each other.

The *Transcript* article noted that Wilson and Davidson were wed on June 22, 1892. The pair was married for more than sixty years. Readers craved stories about couples who found one another using unconventional methods. Happily-ever-after tales of mail-order brides and grooms helped make the mail-order industry popular and gave single men and women who longed for a partner hope that such a life was possible.

Afterword

"It is not good that man should be alone," the Lord said in the book of Genesis. No one knew that better than the lonely bachelors on the American frontier. It is with that in mind that brides—women who wanted an honorable husband—were imported. The absence of women in the Old West and marriageable men in the East led many to participate in unconventional ways to acquire a partner. The advertisements that were placed in mail-order bride publications, as well as the matrimonial agents that were hired between 1853 and 1890, brought many men and women together. Posts placed in newspapers such as the *New Plan Company* catalog and magazines such as *Hand and Heart* conveyed the longing of miners, trappers, and farmers for a spouse and expressed their promises to endeavor to be worthy of any women who accepted their hand in marriage.

A poem that appeared in the March 29, 1878, edition of the Hagerstown, Maryland newspaper the *Hagerstown Mail,* carried the sentiments of one such unattached man.

A Wife Wanted
I want a wife to cheer my life –
I care not if she's such a stunning beauty,
So I but find
That she is kind,
And knows and practices her duty.
I want a wife
A stranger to strife –

A gentle, unaffected creature;
One who can pass
A looking glass
Save stopping to survey each feature.
I want a wife
With vigor and life –
Where nerves are never in a flutter;
Who will not roam,
But stay at home,
And brew, and bake, and make the butter.
I want a wife
Who through her life
Was never known to harm a shirt;
Who'll bring me a recipe
To keep the buttons on a skirt.
If such a one
Dwells beneath the sun,
And don't mind leaving friends behind her,
With the author of this
She'll find true bliss
By informing me where to find her.
—SIMON SINCLAIR

Marriage brokers, keenly aware of the money to be made matching eligible men and women, took full advantage of the situation. Fees for bringing couples together usually ranged from $70 to $400, although some brokers charged more.

Some particularly ambitious entrepreneurial types took matchmaking to a practically wholesale level. Asa Mercer, an entrepreneur residing in Seattle, Washington, organized a project for female immigration. For a $225 fee, Mercer promised suitable wives for men no longer wanting to be single. On January 16, 1866, a group of eligible maids and widows left New York under

Mercer's care aboard the SS *Continental.* The seven-thousand-mile voyage proved to be a success. Mercer fulfilled every contract with more or less satisfaction.

More than twenty years prior to Mercer's trip, Eliza Farnham, an enterprising widow from New York, sought to recruit unencumbered females to join her matrimonial expedition west. She believed the gentling influence of a good woman could bring positive lasting changes for western pioneers and tame the wild frontier. Two hundred ladies responded to Eliza's advertisement, but only a handful agreed to pay the $250 fee and accompany her to California. Upon arriving in San Francisco, Eliza met and married an entrepreneur named William Alexander Fitzpatrick.

According to the majority of ads placed in *Matrimonial News,* the country's leading mail-order bride newspaper in the 1870s, men were searching for women who were musically inclined. They craved the comfort and entertainment value that music offered. Women, on the other hand, sought financial security over all else. They wanted a man who was solvent and could adequately provide for them and their future children. An advertisement addressing those qualities a man would find attractive and those a hopeful maiden needed in a husband, appeared in the fall 1877 edition of the *Matrimonial News:* "Good, honest, respectable widow, strong and healthy, with business ability; age 48, weight 180, height 5 feet 11 inches, blue eyes, light brown hair, nationality French, Protestant religion, personal property worth $500, and also a musician; would marry a good honest man who is not afraid of work and would appreciate a good companion. Would like to hear from men of means."

Critics who objected to mail-order brides argued that such arrangements "cheapened" the sanctity of holy matrimony. Leaders of the Puritan church in Plymouth, Massachusetts, thought the practice would lead to the belief that marrying for love was less important than marrying for economic conditions. Politicians such as Horace Greeley and Protestant clergymen like Henry Ward Beecher believed mail-order brides were necessary given the ratio of women to men on the East Coast.

In January 1873, the *Alton* (IL) *Evening Telegraph* reported that there were between thirty and forty times more women in the city of New York than men. "So long as war, commerce and the demands of the world for male labor exists to the extent in which they are now enjoyed in mining and railroading," the article noted, "to the exclusion of females, women will be more numerous than ever."

BIBLIOGRAPHY

The Busy Bee Club

Brown, Dee. *Wondrous Times on the Frontier.* New York: Harper Collins Publishers, 1991.

Hine, Darlene Clark. *Black Women in America: An Historical Encyclopedia.* New York: Carlson Publishing, 1933.

Katz, William L. *Black Women of the Old West.* New York: Atheneum Books, 1995.

Miller, Brandon M. *Buffalo Gals: Women of the Old West.* New York: Lerner Publications Company, 1994.

Annie Stephens & Asa Mercer

Woods, L. Milton. *Asa Shinn Mercer: Western Promoter & Newspaper.* Norman, OK: The Arthur Clark Company, 2003.

Alton Evening Telegram (Alton, IL), September 27, 1921.

Daily Milwaukee News (Milwaukee, WI), January 26, 1866.

Independent Press Telegram (Long Beach, CA), June 12, 1952.

Logansport Daily Reporter (Logansport, IN), April 7, 2004.

Lowell Daily News (Lowell, IN), October 2, 1949.

The News-Post (Frederick, MD), April 9, 2004.

Hannah Gould

Berton, Pierre. *The Life & Death of the Last Great Gold Rush.* Whitefish, MT: Kessinger Publishing, 2007.

Wilson, Graham. *The Klondike Gold Rush Photographs from 1896–1899.* Whitehorse, Yukon, Canada: Wolf Creek Books, 1997.

Boston Globe, April 13, 1898.

Frank Leslie's Illustrated Weekly (Albany, NY), December 30, 1897.

Morning Record (Avon, OH), November 28, 1897.

Newcastle News (New Castle, PA), December 16, 1897.

New York Times, December 16, 1897.

New York Tribune, August 25, 1897.

World News (New York), October 11, 1897. *World News* (New York), May 1, 1898.

Additional Reference Material

"A Happy Ride," *Nevada County Historical Bulletin* 7, no. 3 (1975).

"A History of Jerome and Surrounding Areas," *Idaho State Historical News* 12 (1951).

Lardner, William, and M. J. Brock. *History of Placer and Nevada Counties.* Los Angeles: Historic Record Company, 1924.

"Marriage Customs in Early California," *Californians Magazine* (November/December 1991).

Albuquerque Morning Journal (Albuquerque, NM), May 18, 1911.

Alton Evening Telegraph (Alton, IL), January 17, 1873.

Alton Evening Telegraph (Alton, IL), September 27, 1921.

Altoona Mirror, Altoona, PA, October 27, 1915.

Anaconda Standard (Anaconda, MT), August 27, 1906.

Anglo American Times (New York), November 12, 1870.

Bismarck Daily Tribune (Bismarck, ND), March 27, 1921.

Boston Daily Globe, November 19, 1886.

Boston Daily Globe, July 17, 1897.

Carroll Daily Herald (Carroll, IA), January 14, 1927.

Coeur d'Alene Press (Coeur d'Alene, ID), June 22, 1914.

Daily Alta California (San Francisco), October 6, 1859.

Daily Light (San Antonio, TX), March 19, 1898.

Daily Republican (Decatur, IL), October 29, 1895.

Daily Tribune (Salt Lake City, UT), February 23, 1891.

Daily Tribune (Salt Lake City, UT), March 15, 1891.

Decatur Review (Decatur, IL), April 16, 1891.

Decatur Review (Decatur, IL), August 25, 1897.
Delphos Daily Herald (Delphos, OH), November 27, 1904.
Denton Journal (Denton, MD), June 21, 1873.
Des Moines Daily News (Des Moines, IA), January 29, 1912.
El Paso Times (El Paso, TX), October 5, 1926.
Eureka Sentinel (Eureka, NV), June 26, 1875.
Evening Post (Denver, CO), November 11, 1904.
Frank Leslie's Illustrated Weekly (Albany, NY), August 7, 1869.
Frank Leslie's Illustrated Weekly (Albany, NY), October 12, 1869.
Hagerstown Mail (Hagerstown, MD), March 29, 1878.
Halcyon Matrimonial Company, 1913.
Harper's Weekly (New York), December 10, 1908.
Hutchinson Daily News (Hutchinson, KS), August 11, 1908.
Hutchinson Daily News (Hutchinson, KS), May 21, 1932.
Indian Journal (Muskogee, OK), March 16, 1887.
Indianapolis Star (Indianapolis, IN), May 31, 1916.
Iowa State Reporter (Waterloo, IA), April 17, 1890.
Jewish Standard (Teaneck, NJ), July 5, 1889.
Joplin New Herald (Joplin, MO), May 17, 1929.
Journal-Tribune (Biddeford, ME), March 29, 1916.
Ladies Home Journal, November 1886.
Lloyd's Weekly London Newspaper, October 19, 1890.
Logansport Daily Reporter (Logansport, IN), June 23, 1890.
Logansport Pharos (Logansport, IN), October 2, 1903.
Matrimonial News (Kansas City, MO), January 8, 1887.
Morning Record (Avon, OH), November 28, 1907.
Muskogee Times-Democrat (Muskogee, OK), November 26, 1915.
New Castle News (New Castle, PA), December 16, 1897.
New York Times, February 20, 1891.
New York Tribune, August 25, 1897.
North Adams Evening Transcript (North Adams, MA), February 10, 1906.
Oakland Tribune (Oakland, CA), April 22, 1913.

Oakland Tribune (Oakland, CA), June 10, 1929.

Ogden Standard Examiner (Ogden, UT), July 14, 1929.

Ogden Standard Examiner (Ogden, UT), October 5, 1931.

Orange County Times Press (Middletown, NY), March 23, 1915.

Pittsburgh Post-Gazette (Pittsburgh, PA), May 14, 1929.

Portsmouth Daily Times (Portsmouth, OH), April 5, 1921.

Salt Lake City Daily Tribune (Salt Lake City, UT), March 15, 1891.

San Francisco Argonaut, May 7, 1892.

Santa Fe New Mexican, March 9, 1920.

Santa Fe New Mexican, February 14, 1988.

Stevens Point Daily Journal (Stevens Point, WI), March 11, 1912.

Syracuse Herald (Syracuse, NY), November 9, 1913.

Syracuse Herald (Syracuse, NY), November 12, 1916.

Syracuse Standard (Syracuse, NY), December 11, 1886.

Washington Post, October 15, 1905.

Washington Post, June 2, 1915.

Waterloo Evening Courier (Waterloo, IA), February 6, 1905.

Waterloo Evening Courier (Waterloo, IA), February 10, 1905.

Waterloo Evening Courier (Waterloo, IA), June 3, 1910.

Week's News (London), May 5, 1877.

World News (New York), December 5, 1890.

World News (New York), May 1, 1898.

INDEX

advertisements, 7
  in mail-order bride
    periodicals, 137
  in *The Matrimonial News*, 78–79
  in newspapers, 119–24
Afflack, Charles K., 127
African Americans, 31–34
Alaska, 114–18
Alford, Cynthia A., 100
American Friendship Society, 28
Anderson, Sara, 33

bachelorettes. *See* single life;
    spinsters; women
bachelors, confirmed, 83, 108–9.
    See also single life
Bagley, Daniel, 45
Bailey, John R., 123
Baines, Sara, 103–7
Baker, E. C., 114
Balzac, Barbara, 37–39
bank clerk
  accidentally matched with aunt,
    18–20
beards, 121–22
Berry, William J., 30
bigamy, 3–6, 28–29
Brandon, Eva, 63–66
Brane, Shyon, 1
Braut, Barbara and Margaretha,
    51–52
breach of promise, 111, 125
brides. *See also* women
  advertisements for, 7
  dowries, 54
  jilted, 21–23, 51–52
  merchandise for, 104–7
  photographs, 80
  runaway (*See* runaway brides)

bride ships, 43
bridesmaids, 106
Brinson, Emily, 33
Burch, Blanche, 28
Burden, William H., 122–23
Burke, Lulu, 28–29
Busy Bee Club, 30–34

catalogs, 119
church weddings, 104
City of Columbia, 114–18
clothing and shoes, 104, 106–7.
    See also wedding gowns
Collins, Edith, 88–94
Conant, Roger, 45
Coon, Margaret, 123
correspondence brides. *See* mail-
    order marriages
courting rituals, 52–54, 81–82
cowboys, 98, 132, 134–35
Crescent Hotel and Spa, 60, 62
C. S. Morey Mercantile
    Company, 104
customs, courting and wedding,
    52–54

Davidson, Cydra, 140–41
Detter, Thomas, 33
DeWitt, Minnie May, 128–29
dining, fine, 132–36
divorce, 26–27, 27–28, 57, 111,
    126, 127, 128
dowry, 54
dresses, wedding. *See* wedding
    gowns
Duncan, Leslie Fraser, 7, 8–10, 20,
    108–13

East, lack of men in, 35

education, 36
elopement, 51
Endres, Mary, 28
Everett, Frank, 129–30

farmers, 98
Farnham, Eliza, 144
fashion, 60
finances, 39–40, 84
Fitzpatrick, William A., 144
Fore, Wone, 123–24
Frank Leslie's Illustrated Weekly,
    103, 115, 116, 117

Ganabrant, George C., 127
Gayle, Annie, 2–6
Gold Rush, 2, 115
Gould, Hannah, 114–18
Gould, Kate, 116
Grey, Marie E., 130–31
grooms. *See also* men
    advertisements for, 7
    jilted, 122–23, 125–26 (*See also*
        runaway brides)
Gulless, Eliza, 137–39
Guy, J. E., 130–31

Haans, Elizabeth, 74–76
Halcyon Matrimonial Company,
    50, 127
Hamilton, Cora, 28
Hand and Heart Magazine, 98,
    100–102, 125, 142
happily-ever-after tales, 137–41
Harper's Weekly, 44, 104
Harvey, Fred, 132–36
Harvey Girls, 132–36
Haskin, Frederic J., 101–2
Hemsley, Jay, 103–7
Henderson, Margaret, 116, 118
holidays, romantic, 137

homicide, 63–66
honeymoons, 60, 62, 106
Hope, John, 21

immigrants, 123–24
independence, financial, 39–40

Kaborchev, Edgar, 48
Kent, Eliza, 130
King, Henry Clay, 126
Kish, Edith, 126–27
Kissel, John, 126–27
Kline, Simon, 120–21
Knapp, Horace, 2–6
Knowles, Gladys, 108, 109–13
Kurth, Ava, 55–57

Lafferty, Margaret, 121–22
Leen, Fong Jean, 123–24
Liggett, Utha, 28–29
Linton, Thomas L., 100
loneliness, 95, 142

mail-order marriages. *See also*
    marriage
    critics of, 144–45
    and divorce (*See* divorce)
    funny stories about, 120–22
    jilted brides or grooms, 122–23
    and murder, 63–66
    risks of, 127–28
    statistics about outcome, 97
    successful, 88–95, 100–101,
        131, 137–41
Malin, Richard, 8
Marney, Samuel A., 47
marriage. *See also* mail-order
    marriages
    how to make it successful, 39
    prearranged, 33–34
    statistics, 35–36

marriage brokers, 1, 48–54, 95–102, 108
  critics of, 99
  fees, 50–51, 143
  in foreign countries, 52–54
  and scams, 95
  statistics about, 96
Marshal, Mary, 100–101
matchmakers. *See* marriage brokers
Match Making Magistrate, 97
matrimonial clubs, 67–77
Matrimonial News, The, 7–21, 129
  advertisements, 78–79, 144
  bank clerk accidentally matched with aunt, 18–20
  features of, 58–62
  and Leslie Duncan, 108–13
  misleading ads, 126–27
  personal ads, 10, 12–13
  photographs in, 8, 9, 11, 14, 61
  sample ads, 13–17
  and successful marriages, 137
  why it was so popular, 78–79
McGover, Leola, 27–28
men. *See also* bachelors, confirmed; grooms
  income and marriage, 38
  married to multiple wives, 3–6, 28–29
  personal ads in *The Matrimonial News*, 12–13
  what they want in a mate, 10, 36–40
Mercer, Asa, 41–47, 143–44
merchandise, bridal, 104–7
Miller, Robert, 130
miners and mining, 31–34, 114
Moore, William, 88–94
Morgan, J. W., 74–76
Muntle, Louise, 81–82

murder, 63–66

New Plan Company catalog, 27, 67–77, 142
  misleading ad, 126
  personal ads, 69–70, 73–74
  photographs, 72, 75
  and successful marriages, 137
newspapers, 7
  want ads, 119–24

O'Brien, Pat, 121–22
Oskar, Otto Fredrich, 51–52

Pacific Matrimonial Bureau, 55
Patrick, Wellington, 33
Patterson, Peter, 79, 81–82
periodicals, mail-order bride, 119, 125
  impact of successful connections, 137
  risks of, 127–28
Perkins, Martin, 137–39
personal ads, 69–70, 73–74
  in *The Matrimonial News*, 10, 12–17
  risks of, 127–28
photographs, 19, 68, 71, 75, 80, 107
  in *The Matrimonial News*, 8, 9, 11, 14, 61
  in *New Plan Company* catalog, 72, 75
picture brides, 101–2
poison, 64, 66
poverty, 83, 84

Rablen, Carroll B., 63–66
Ray, J. A., 128–29
restaurants, 132–36
Richardson, Alice, 120–21

Rogers, Will, 133
runaway brides, 122–23, 125–31

San Francisco, CA, 33, 55, 63,
    101, 144
Santa Fe Railroad, 133, 136
scams, 95
Seattle, WA, 42, 46, 117, 118,
    143–44
shaving, 121–22
Sinclair, Simon, 143
single life, 83–87
Sleet, Joe, 24–27
smuggling, 46
social reform, 31
Southard, Bessie, 126
spinsters, 32, 36, 83, 86
SS *Continental*, 41–42, 144
Stephens, Annie, 41–47
Stevens, George, 28–29

thefts, 127
Thompson, Lulu Douglas, 122–23
Thumann, Emma, 51–52
tobacco products, 120–21
trousseau, 106–7, 109

Valentine's Day, 137

Wallace, Nellie, 24–27
want-ad brides, 119–24
wedding gowns, 37, 104, 106
weddings
    customs around the world,
        52–54
    elaborate, 33
    on horseback, 33
    photographs of, 107
Wells, Kate Gannett, 39–40

West
    attempts to refine and civilize,
        132–36
    frontier weddings, 104
    lack of women in, 35, 103
    and loneliness, 142
    women emigrating to, 41–47
White, Frank E., 55–57
Whyte-Melville, Harriet, 111
widows, 38–39, 120, 144. *See also*
    women
Williamson, Clyde, 125–26
Williamson, Pauline, 34
Wilson, Joshua, 139–41
Wohlscleged, Winfred, 100–101
women. *See also* brides; spinsters;
    widows
    African American, 31–34
    auctioned as wives, 116
    college-educated, 36
    cultured, 132–36
    desire for financial security, 144
    emigration to West, 41–47,
        143–44
    and financial independence,
        39–40
    how to find and keep a
        husband, 38
    musically talented, 144
    in New York City, 145
    personal ads in *The Matrimonial
        News,* 13
    pressure to find husbands, 49
    reasons for not marrying, 83–86
    unmarried, 1860–1880, 35
    what they want in a mate, 10,
        36–40
    widowhood, 38–39
Woodring, Lawrence, 27–28

About the Author

Chris Enss has been writing about women of the Old West for more than a dozen years. She loves western culture and travels quite extensively, collecting research for her books. She received the Spirit of the West Alive award, cosponsored by the *Wild West Gazette*, celebrating her efforts to keep the spirit of the Old West alive for future generations. She currently lives in a historic gold-mining town in northern California.